AMRITA DAS

Hope is a Girl Selling Fruit

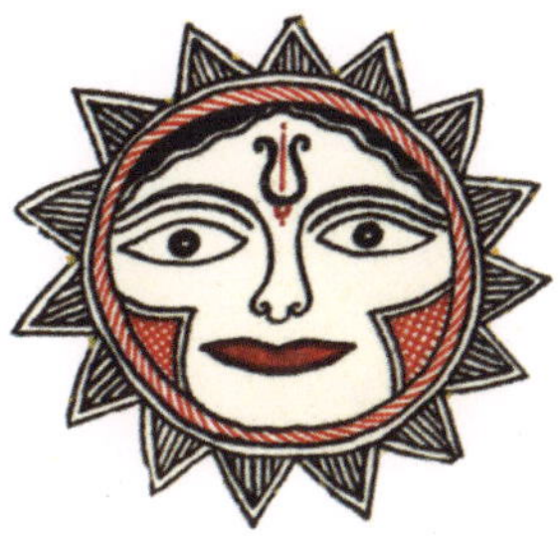

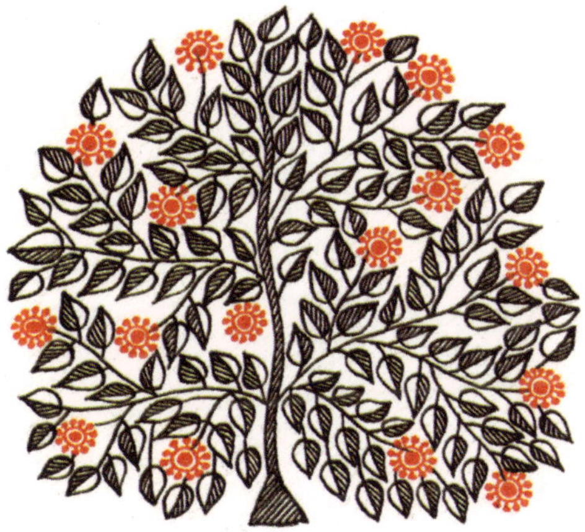

I started out not knowing much,
certainly not about the outside world.
I could paint, but apart from that
there was not much I could do.
And then it came my way,
that sliver of a chance which has
made it possible
for me to do this book.

Life is strange –
you never know what awaits you.

IT ALL STARTED with my journey to Chennai, to attend a book making workshop. I had never travelled so far, and I wasn't sure what to expect.

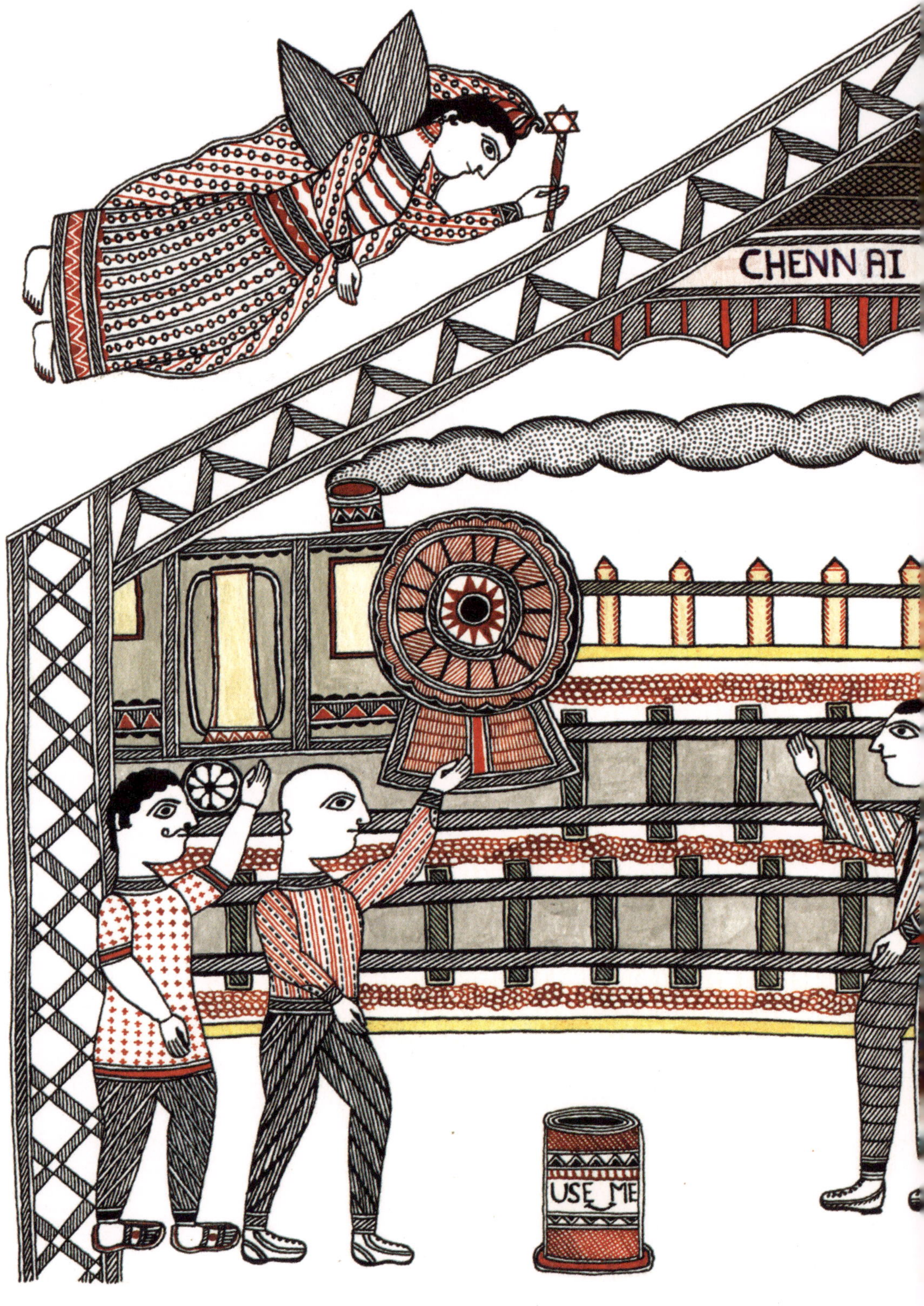

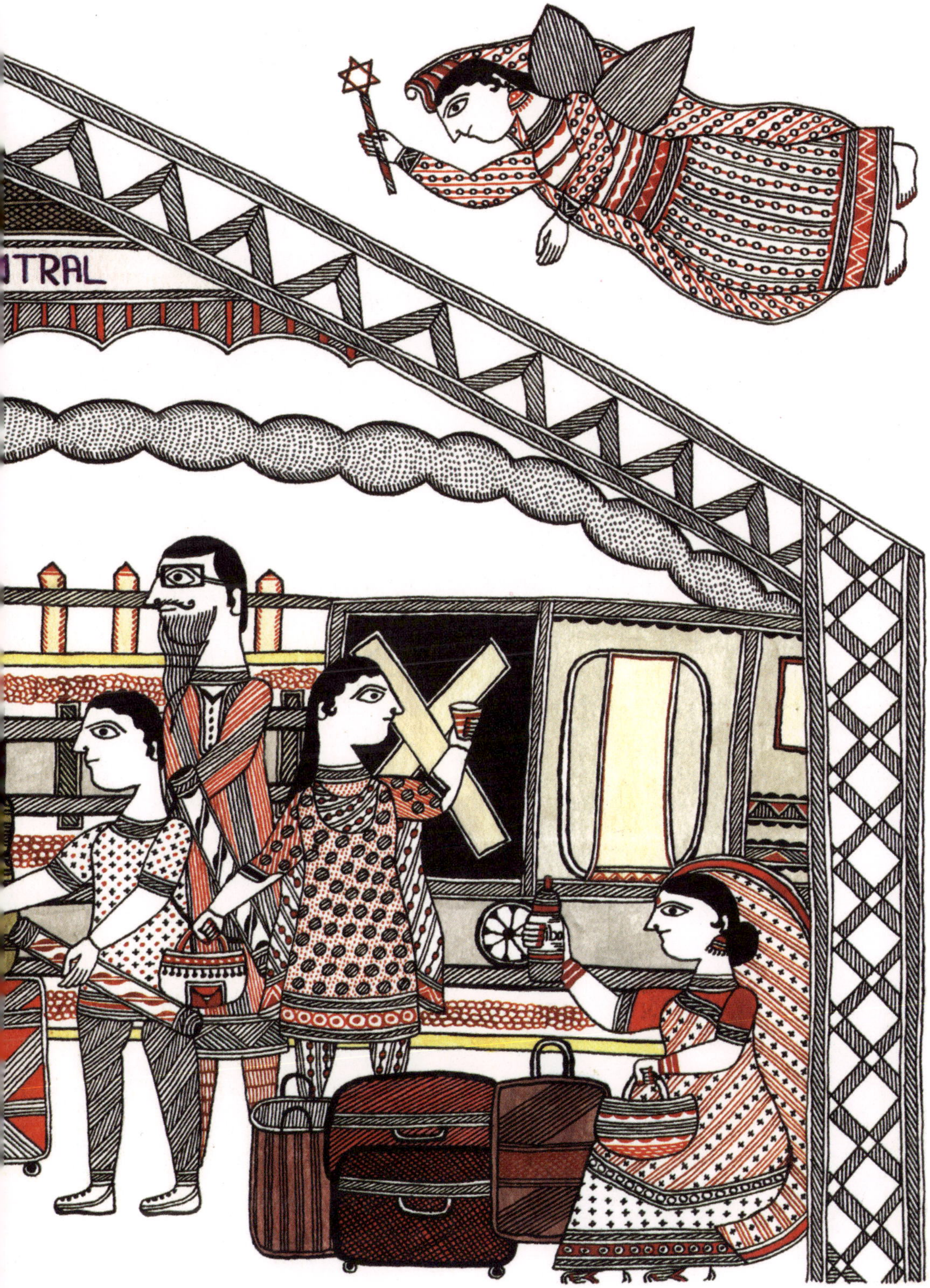

Coming to the small town of Madhubani to learn art was about as far as I got from my village. Even that seemed a distant place at the time.

But I did find a teacher, whose ideas and art I loved and there I began to learn to paint in my own way.

AT THE WORKSHOP,
I was asked to think of a story to draw. I didn't know where to start. I wanted to draw women, but what story would these women be part of?

I thought of my own childhood and started to paint two girls under a tree.

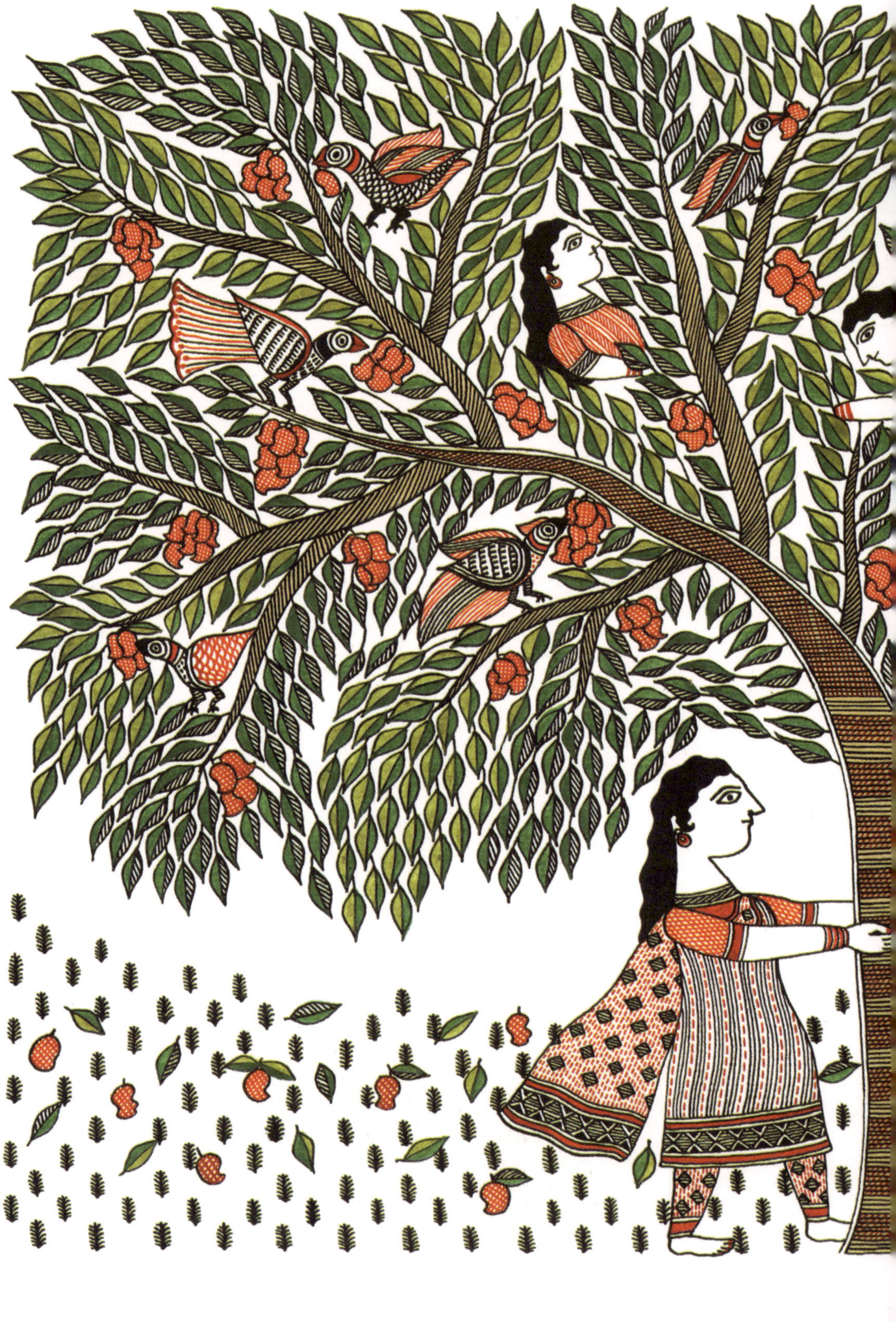

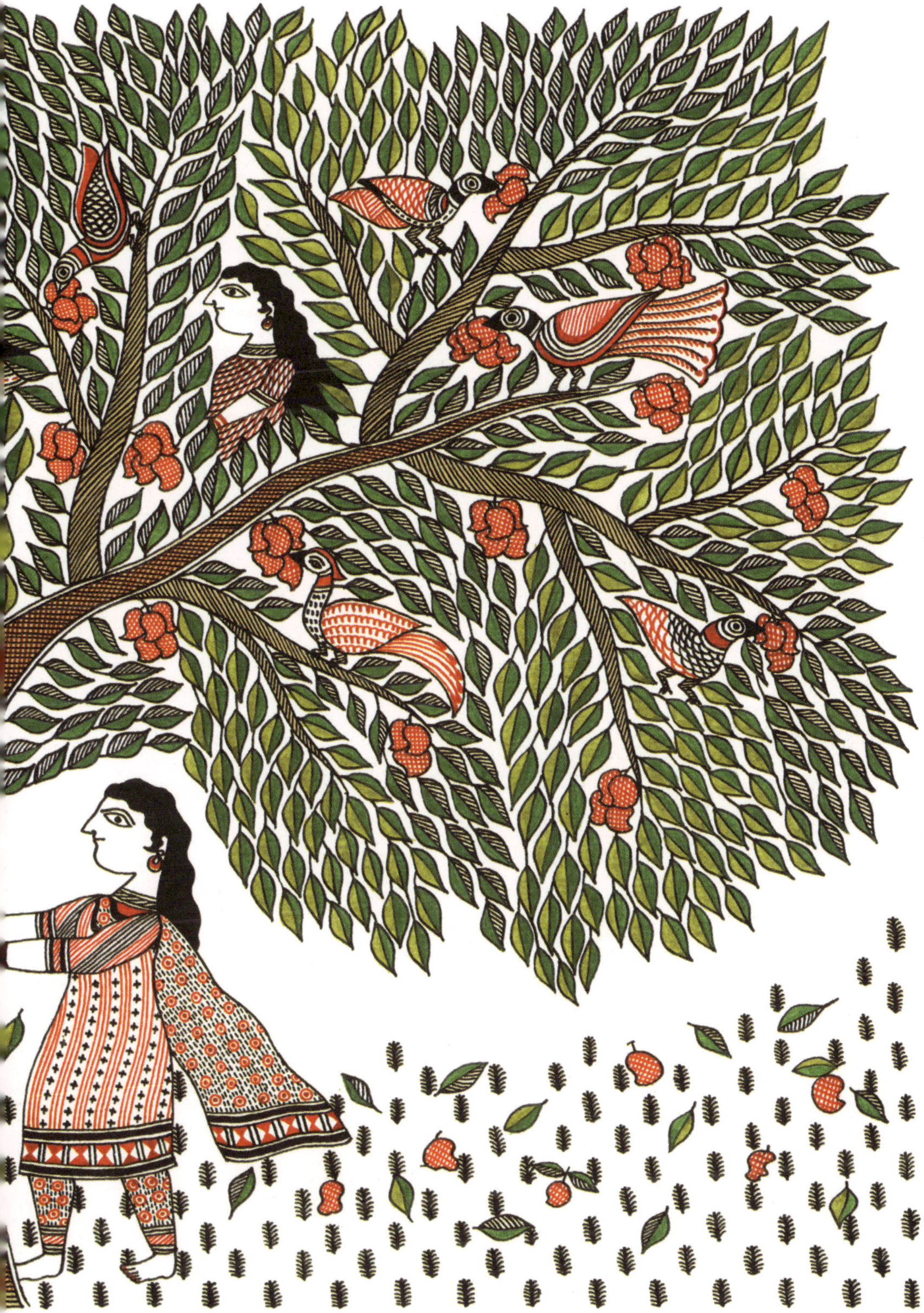

Here they are: they're dancing, happy to be jumping on the leaves. Everything's green, the leaves rustle pleasantly, the birds chirp. It's an idyllic scene.

But was my childhood really like that? Was this the truth?

CHILDHOOD. Mine was far from idyllic, though not untypical. I was responsible for a great deal when I was very small, and my girlhood passed even before I knew it.

So where did that leave my story? I struggled with myself, talked things over with my friends and teacher, who were also part of the workshop. But all I had were ideas, nothing concrete.

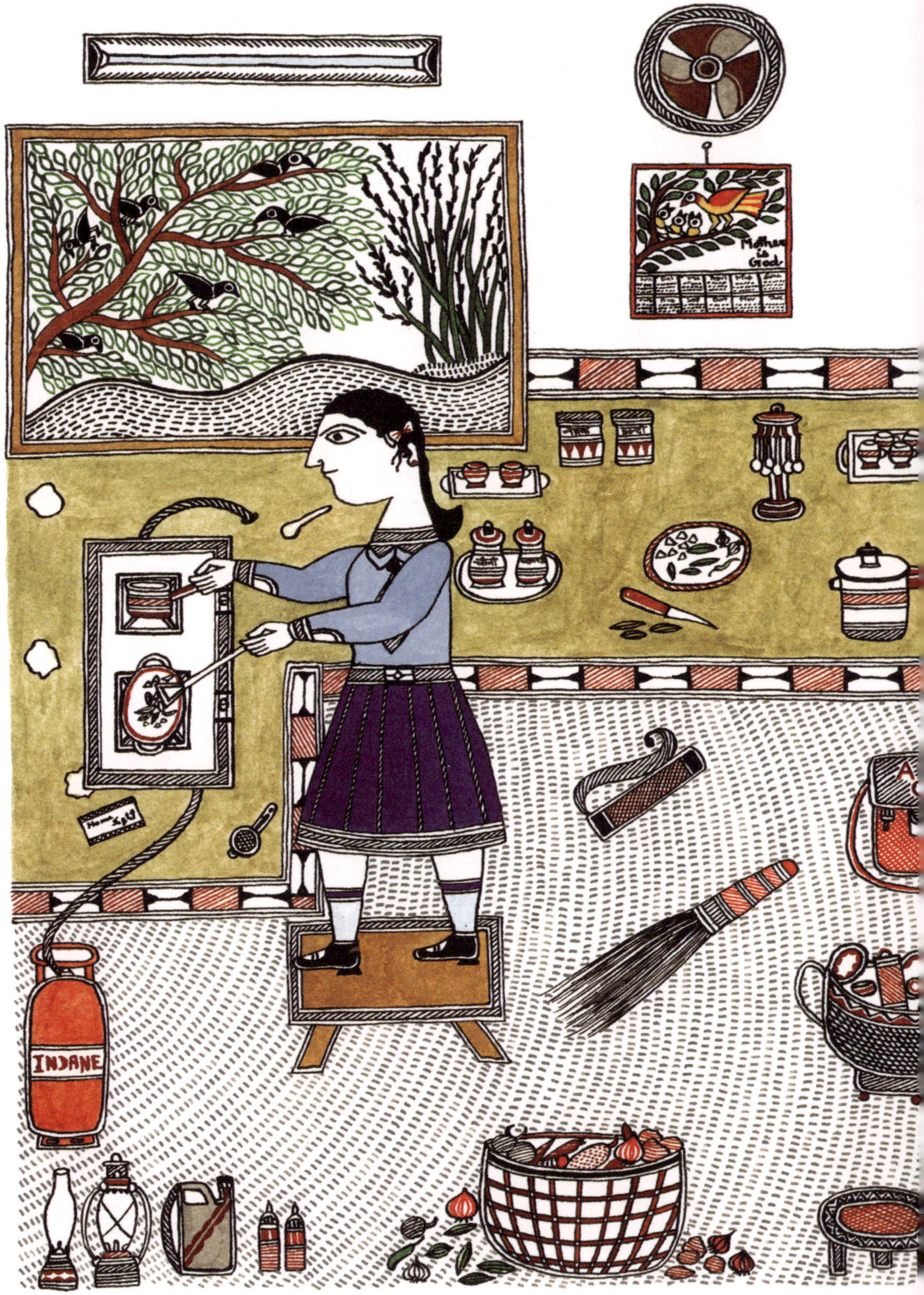

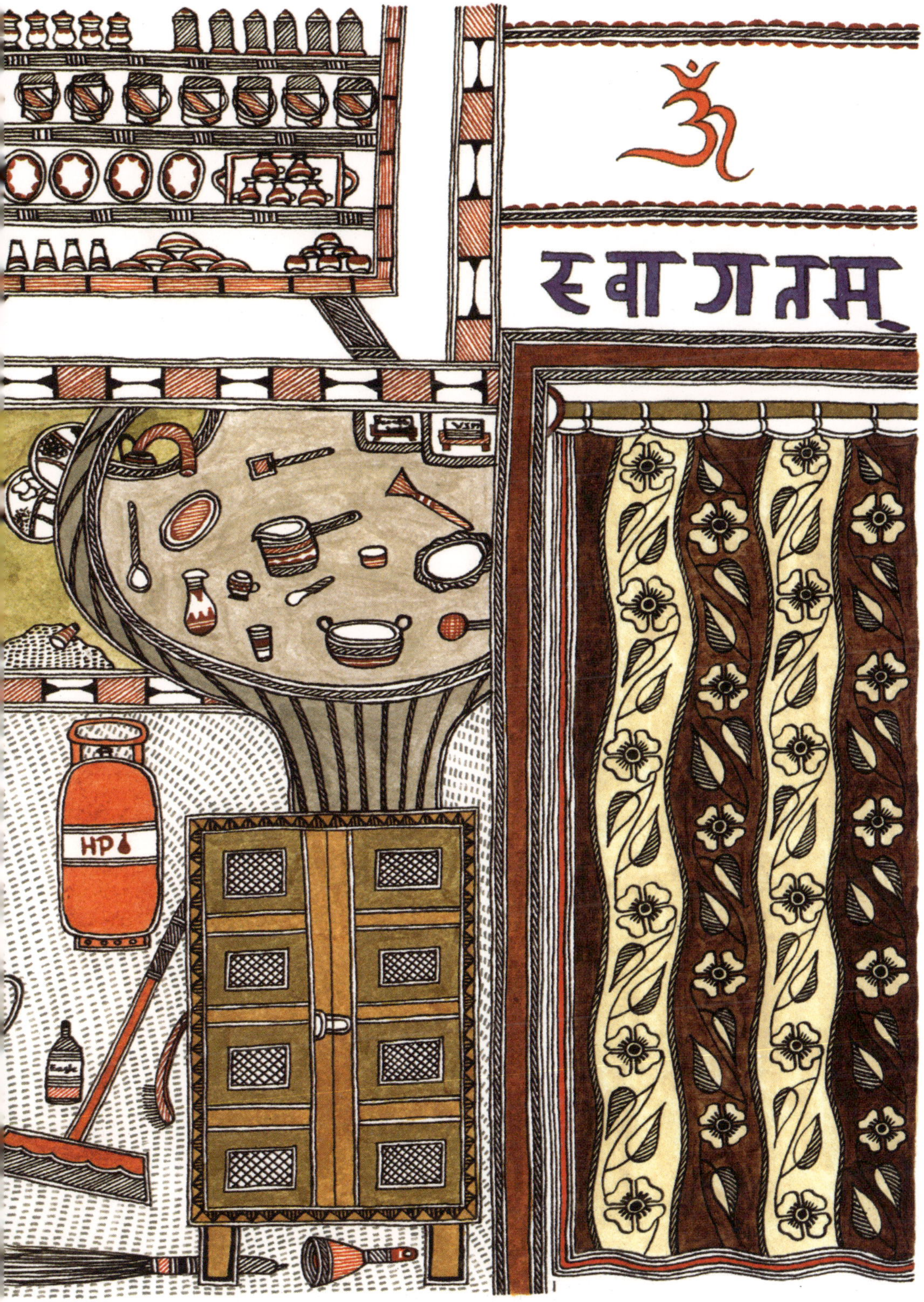

Then suddenly, out of nowhere, I thought of the girl on the train to Chennai.

Of course! I knew, at that moment, how I was going to tell my story. It is her story too.

IT ALL STARTED when I met that girl's eyes: poor, innocent eyes that said so much, even while she was so silent. I saw her going up to her berth in the train, almost as soon as she got on.

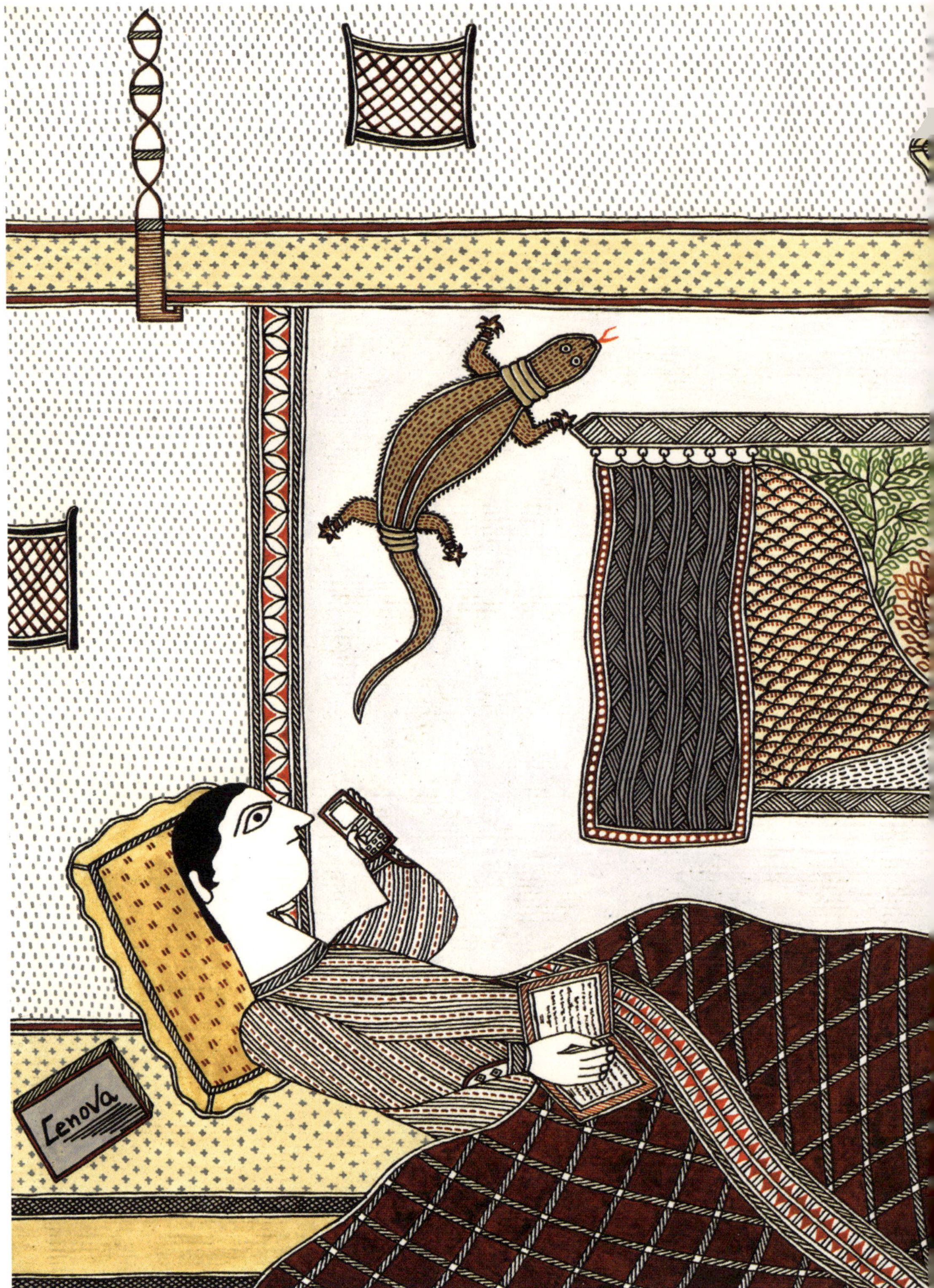

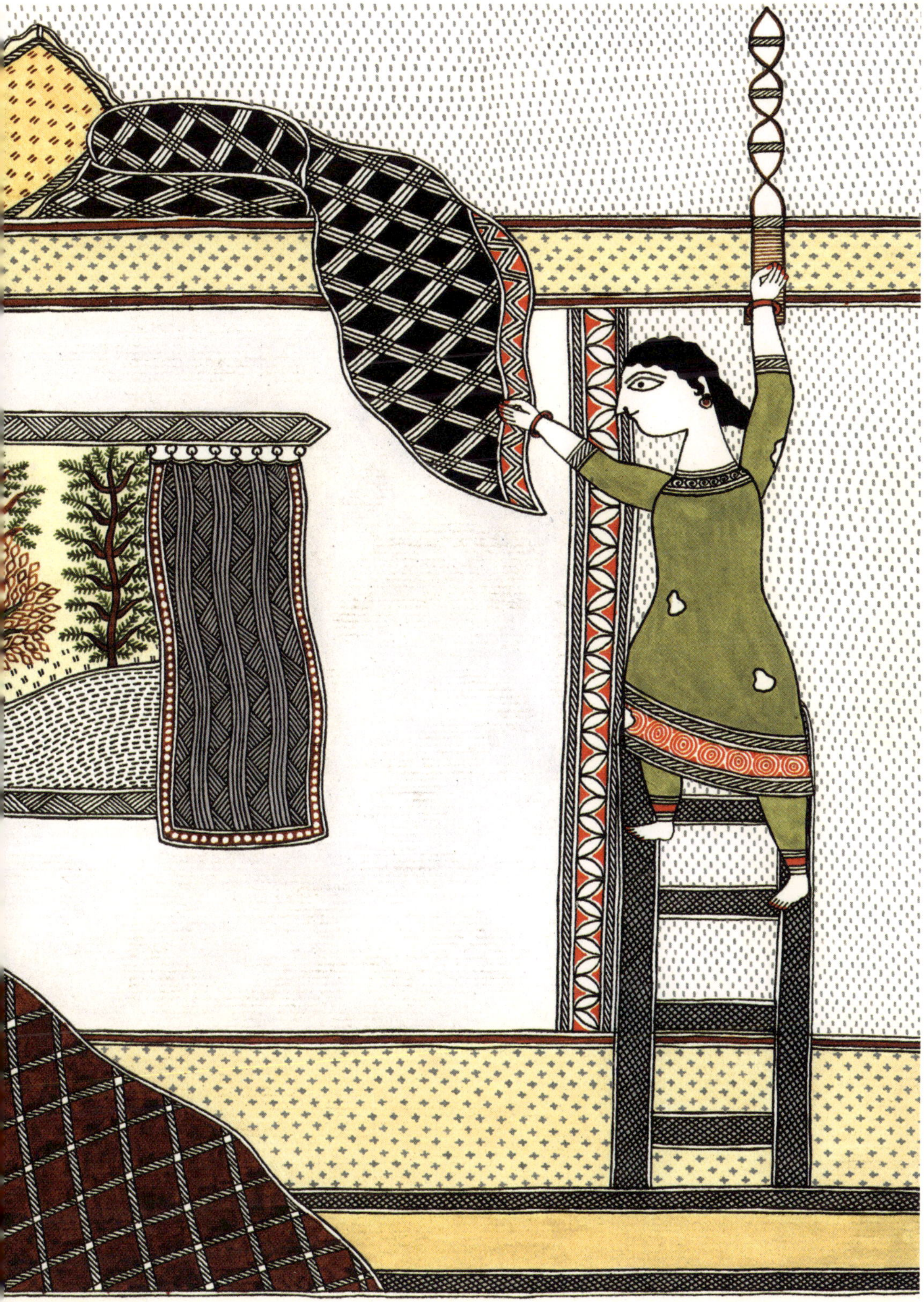

She stayed up there, not eating and I found myself wondering who she was, where she was going… why was she alone?

THERE WE ALL WERE, eating and talking, and I wondered if I should invite her to share our meal. Poor though she was, I felt that she might not like it, if I did.

The poor do have pride. They don't ask, and they have nothing to offer in return.

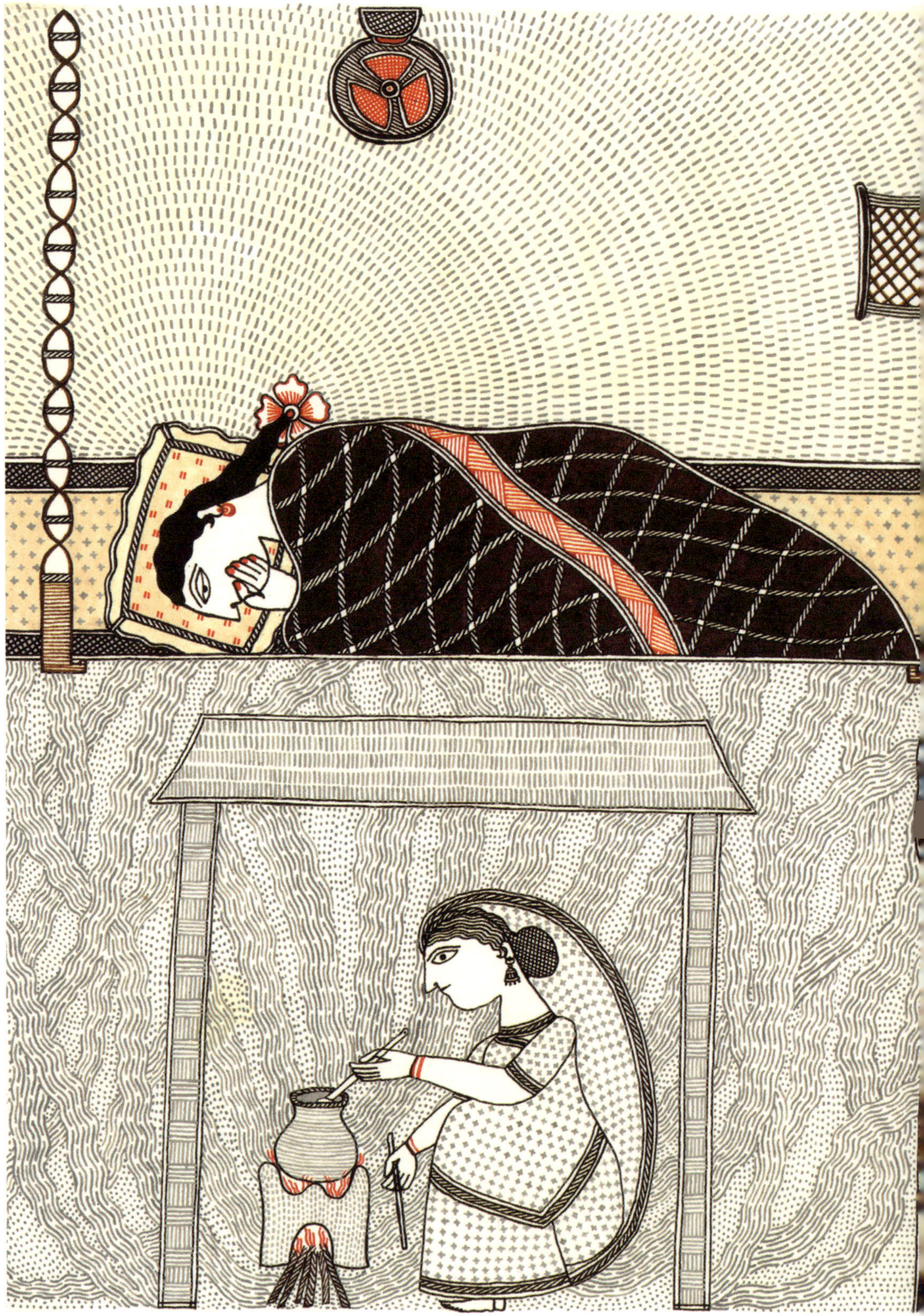

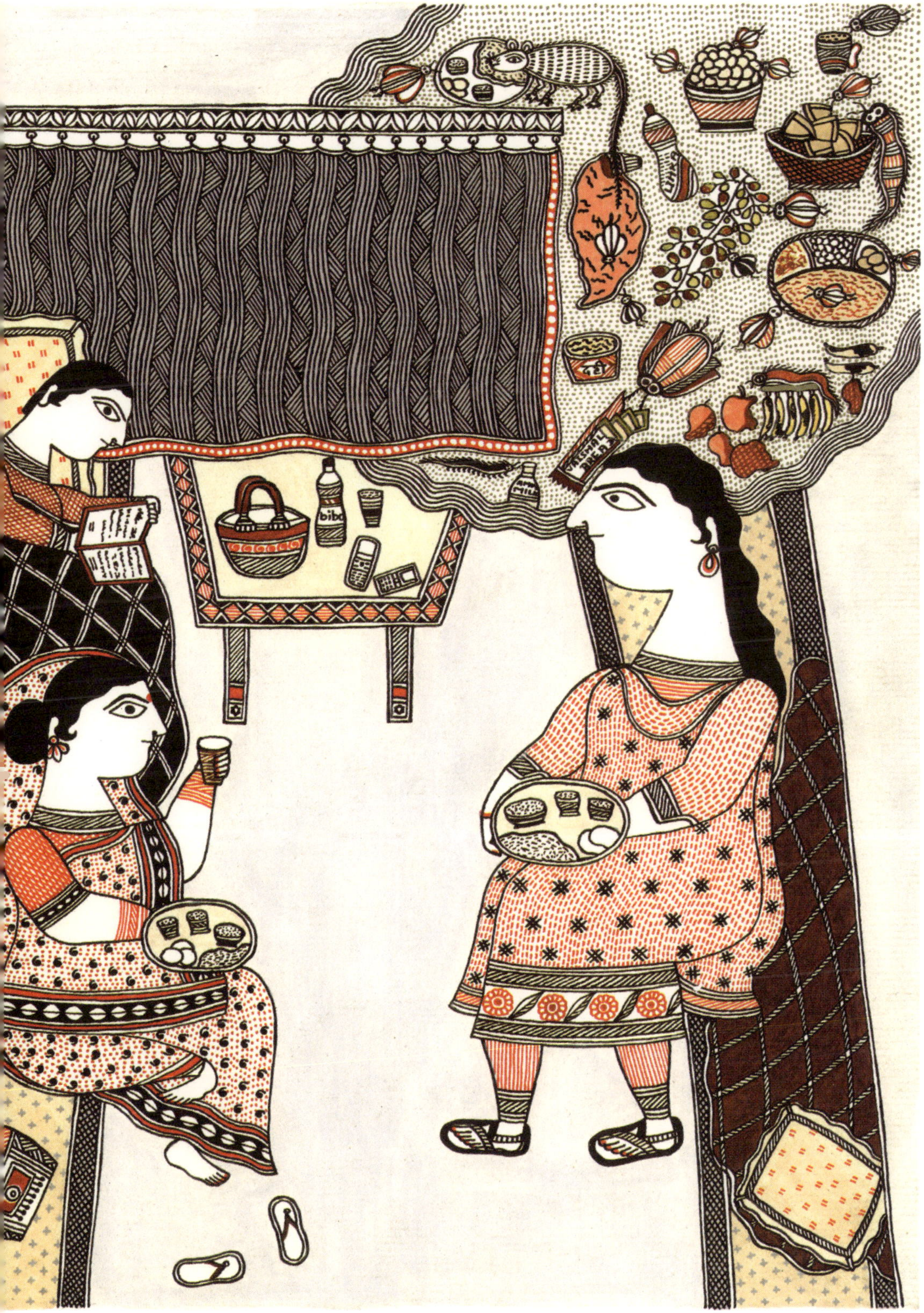

The smell of food must have floated up to her. My mind darted here and there – how could she go to sleep, with nothing in her stomach?

The first night on the train, well past midnight, I woke up and looked for her. She was not there! I panicked.

Scenes from the last movie I'd seen floated before me – girls being kidnapped, sold, trafficked…

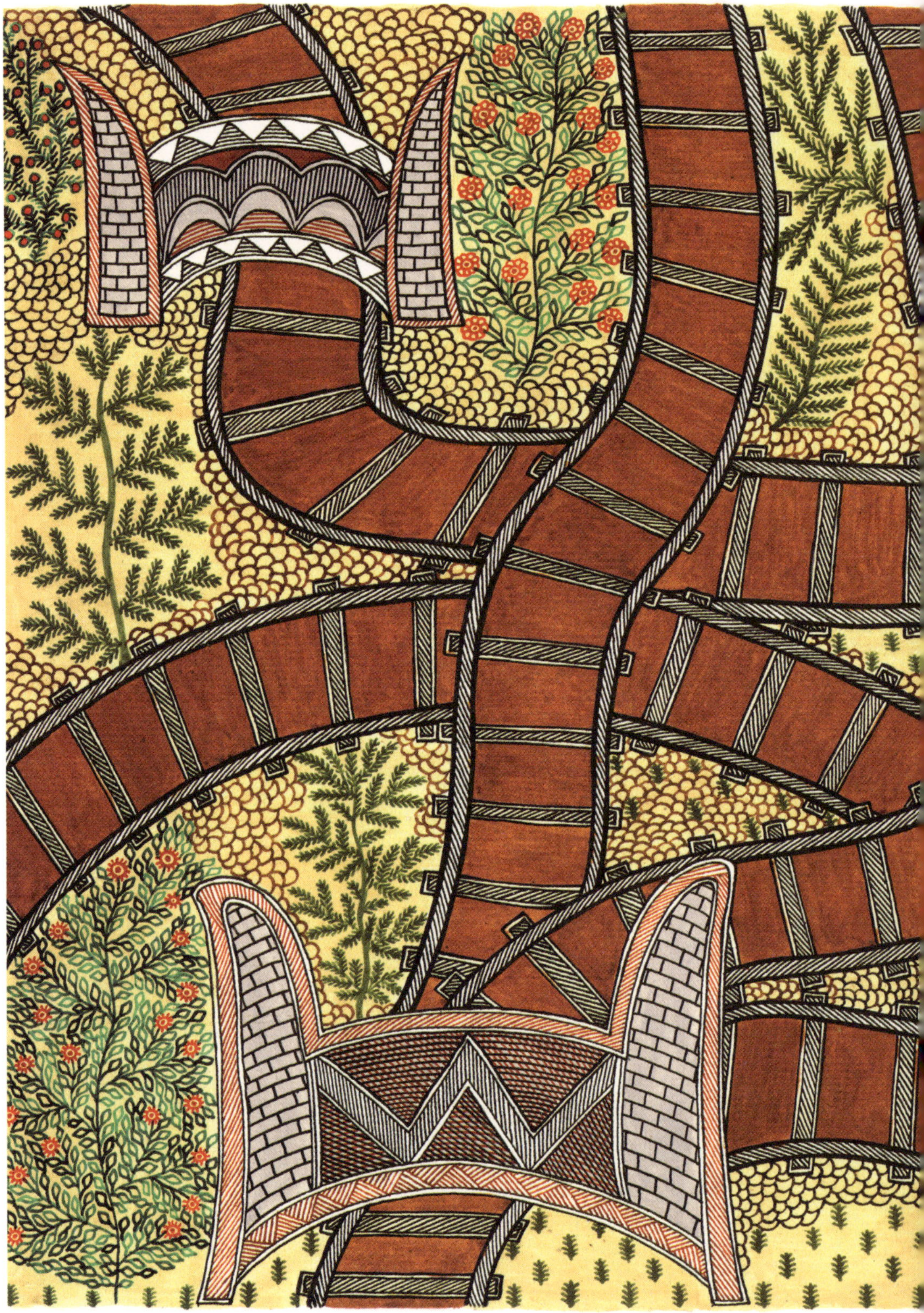

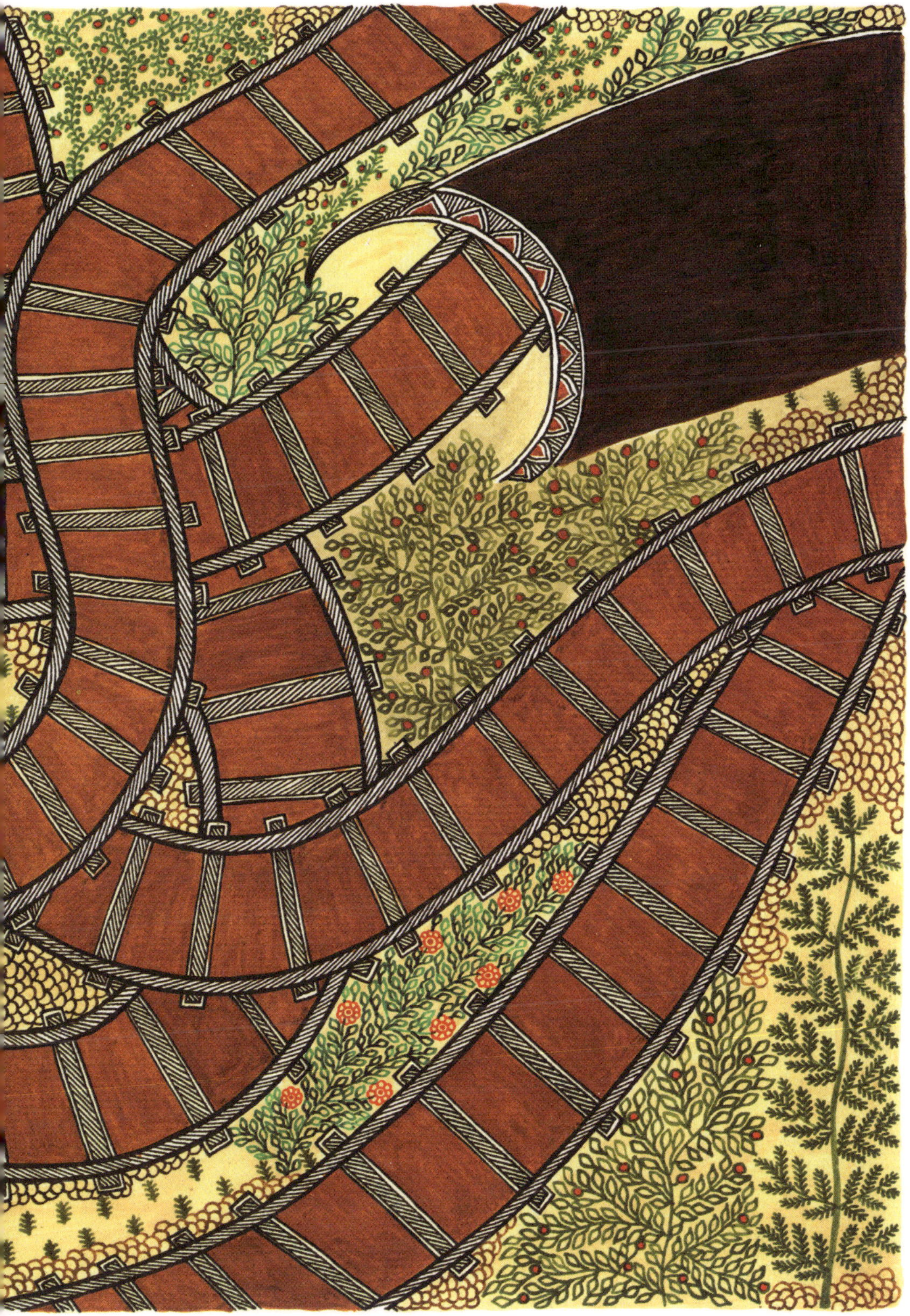

I calmed myself down, thinking: she's just got off, someone must have been waiting at a station for her… maybe she has a real place to go to.

In the morning, she was there again. She had a bit of food with her. Someone had given her something. I was glad, she did have someone to call her own.

THE RICH GO THEIR WAY and are what they are. I don't really care to know them, I'm not drawn to them. But the poor… I've always felt at home with them.

So I tried talking to her. She didn't say much.

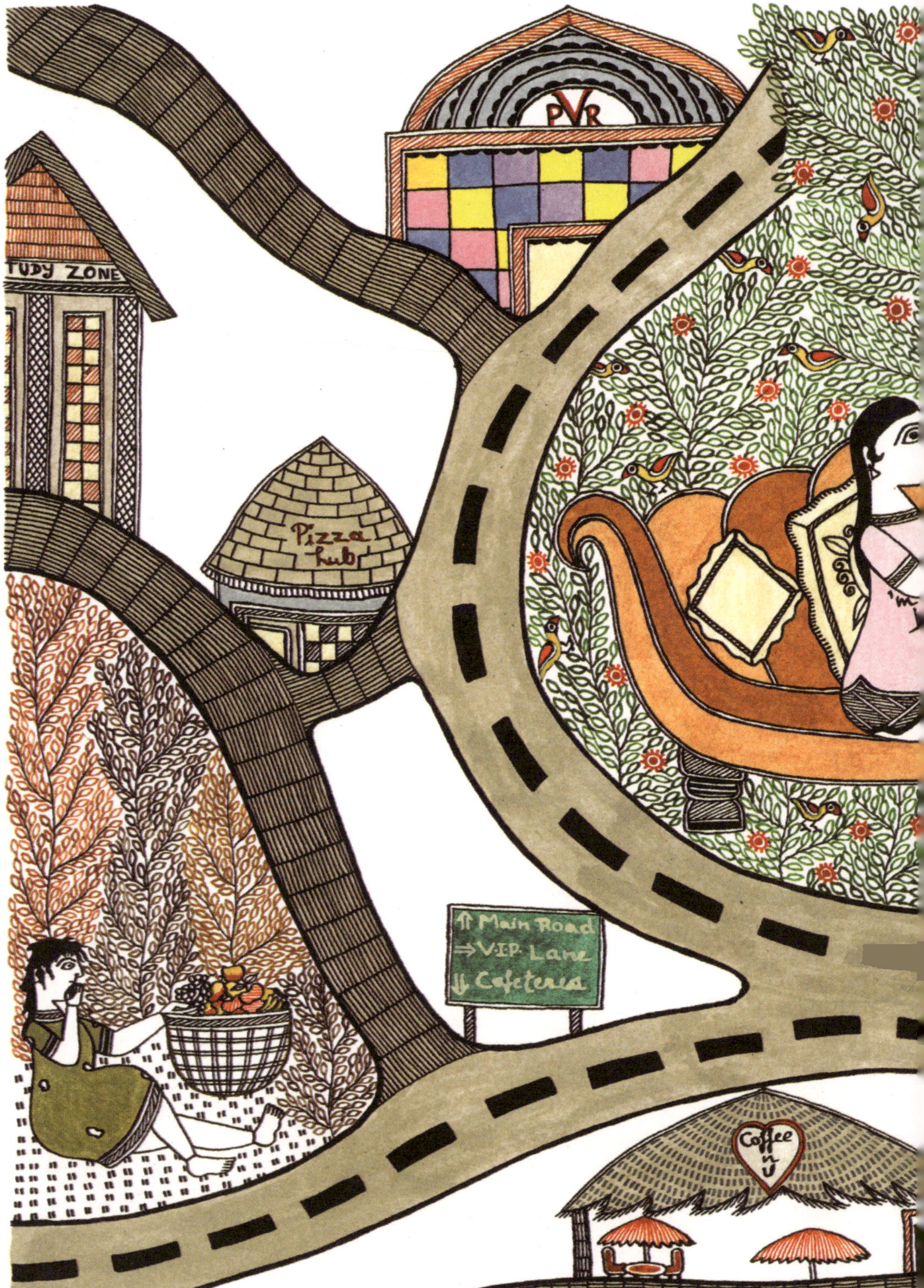

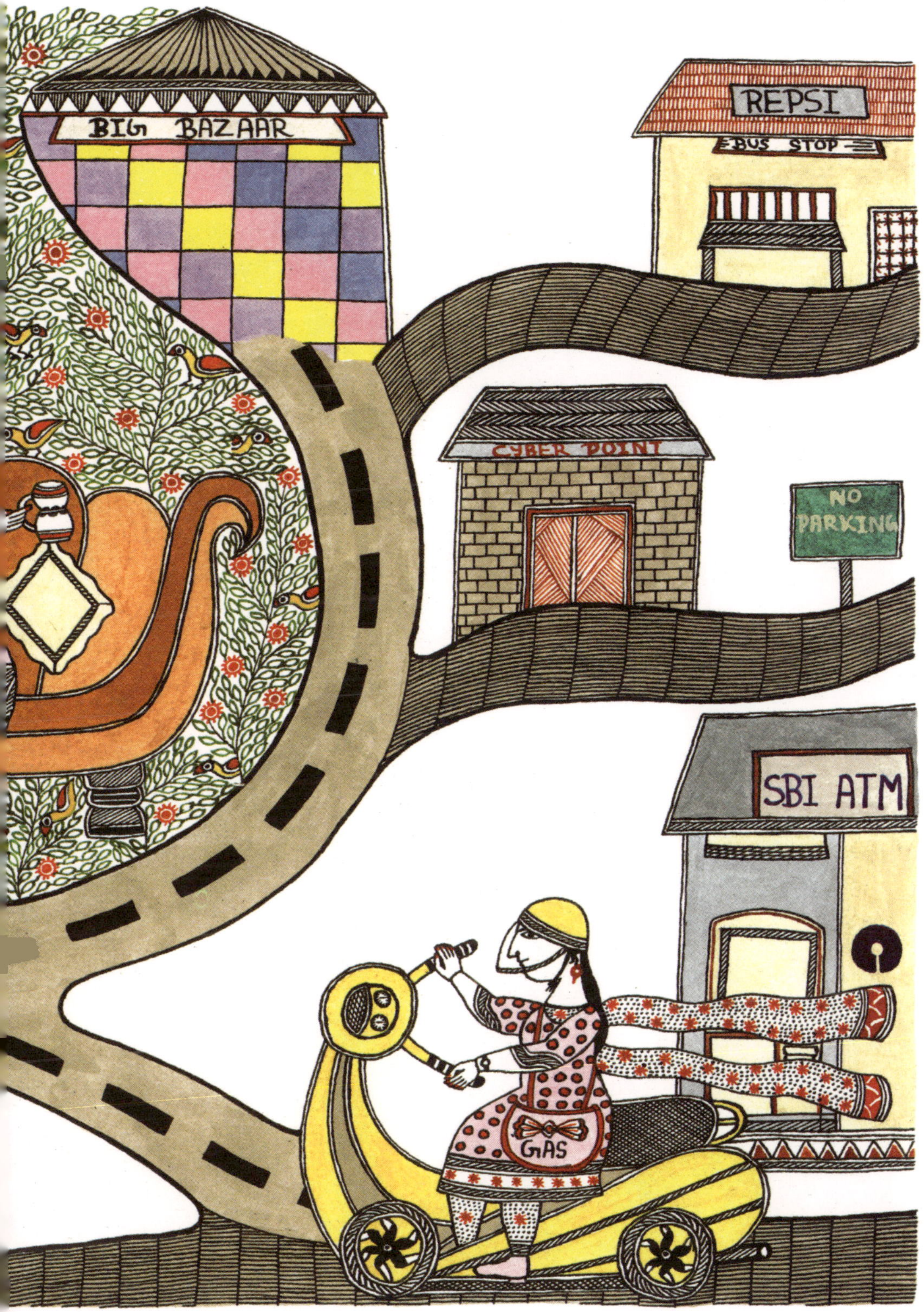

I gathered that she might be going to work in the city at someone's house, as a maid, a household helper.

She knew very little, couldn't have seen much. She probably hadn't gone to school. An address? Does she know where she's going, among all the dense concrete?

A GIRL'S LIFE IS HARD, especially if you're cursed to be poor. It's gone even before you start on it. There's all the work, but even more than being tied to these endless tasks, it's the mean hurtful way people speak to you.

If you dream for a moment, you're asked why you're twiddling your thumbs.

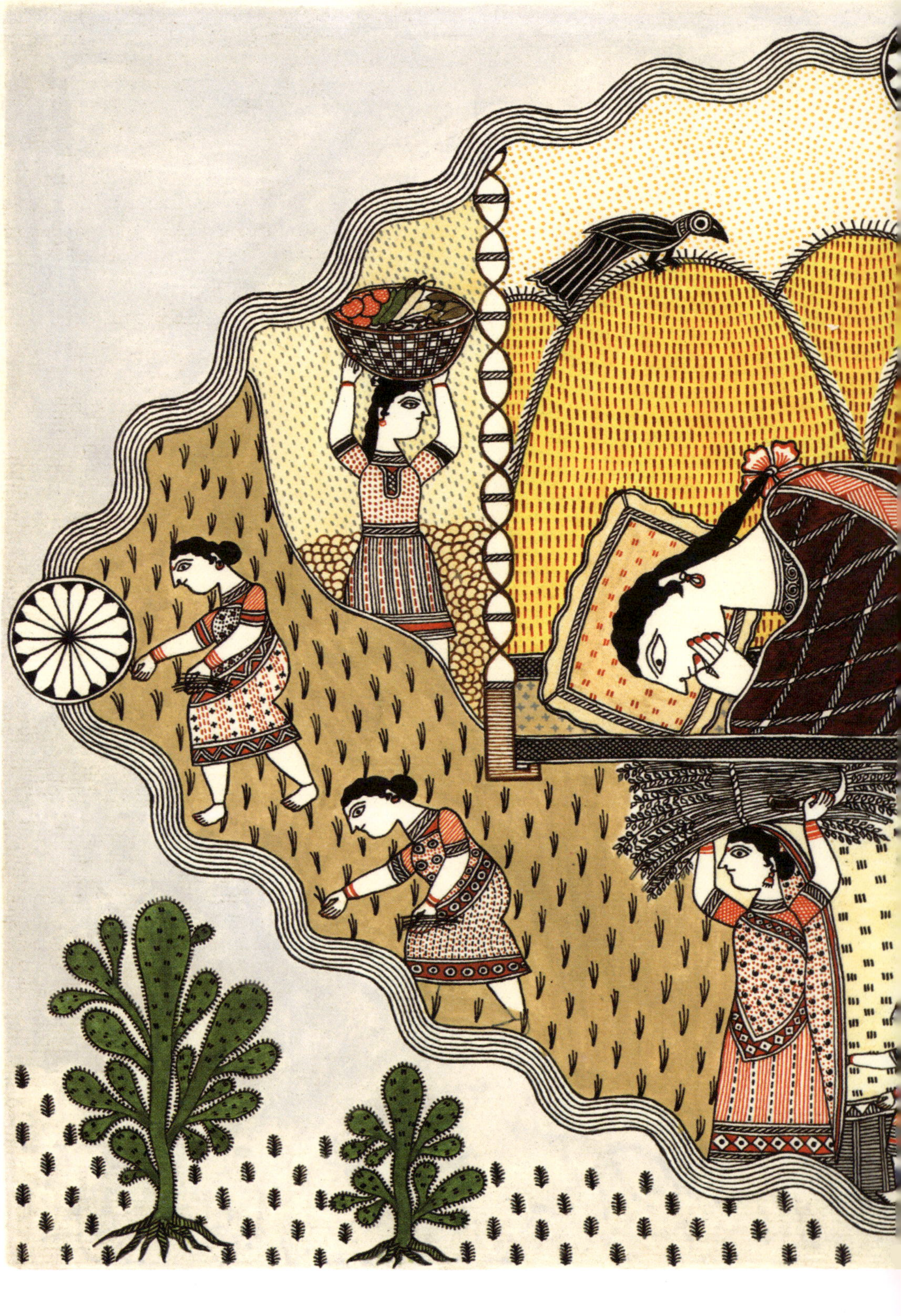

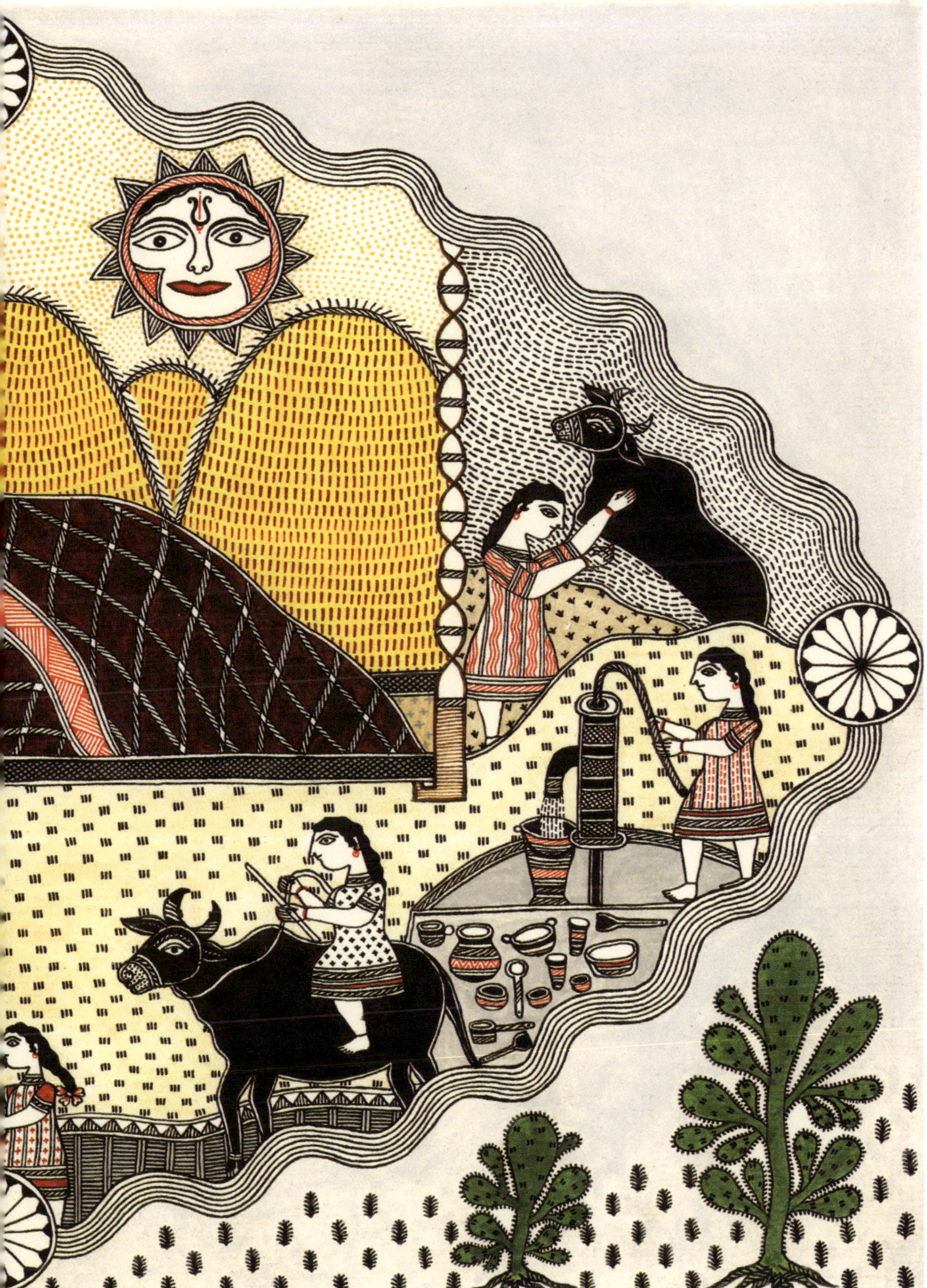

You're not supposed to want anything, let alone allow your heart or your self to travel. No one lets you forget that you're born a girl, not a boy.

Freedom. What does that word mean to us? Going to school? Learning? And then? Marriage? Does that set you free?

THIS GIRL must have dreamt too. She must have let her heart travel. She didn't say much, so I found myself watching her a lot of the time.

She does smile, now and then. Is there a haunted look about her? Are her eyes trusting?

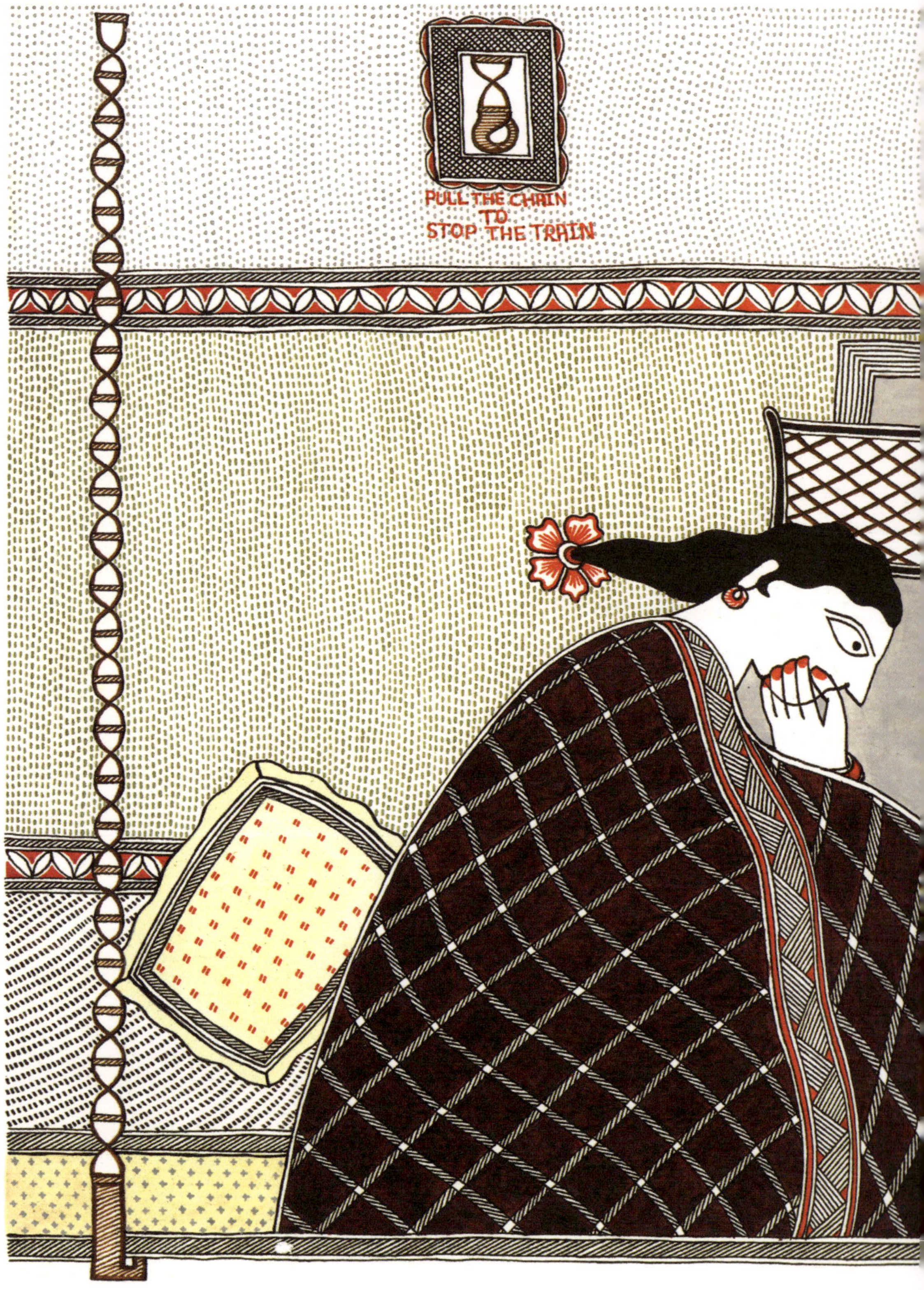

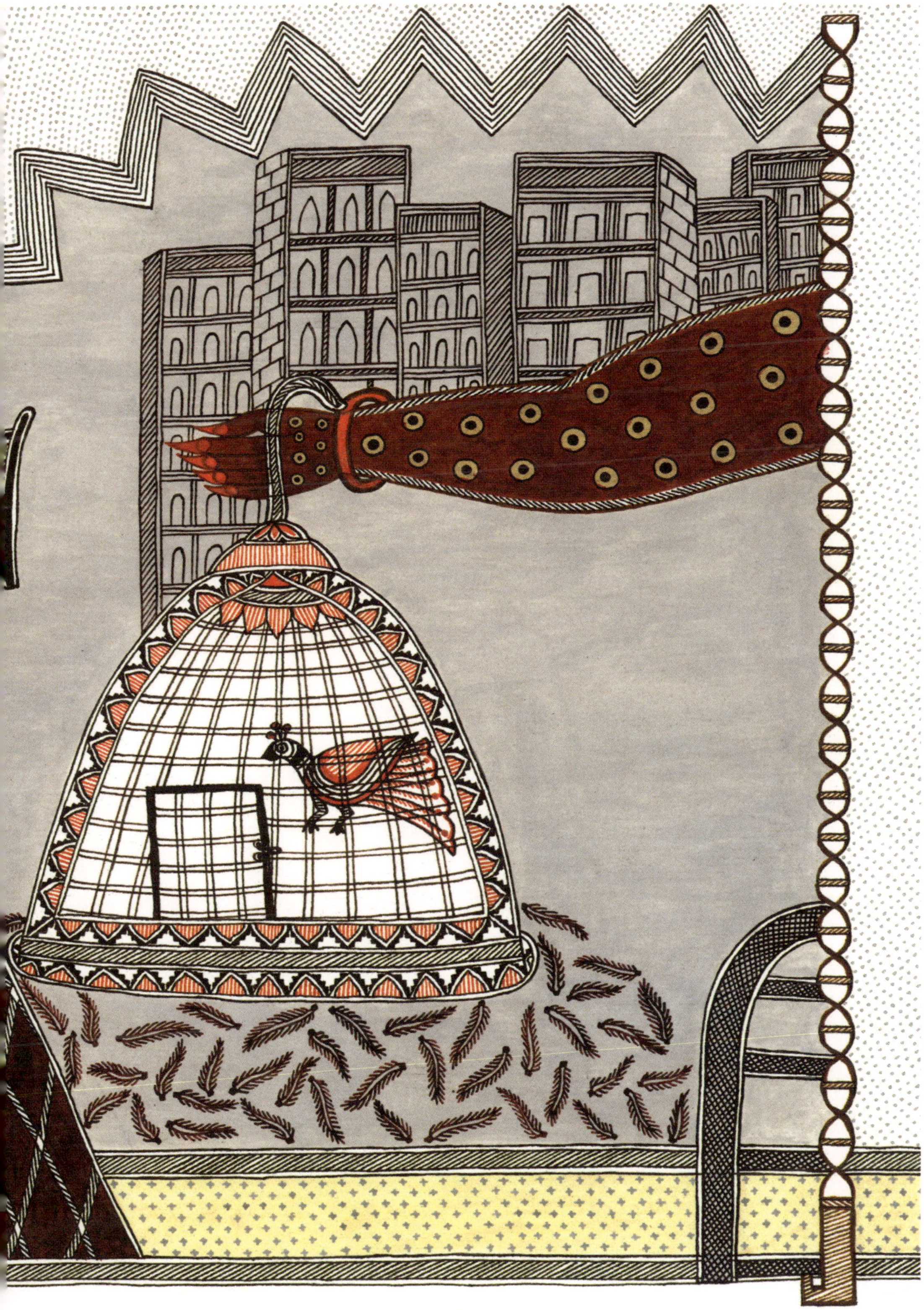

I think that she's like a bird, a delicate bird in an invisible cage. If you were to open the door, she might fly away into freedom. Or maybe she would hesitate, not knowing where to go.

Perhaps this is not what she is all about at all. This is my sense of her.

I WAS SO ABSORBED in this girl that I hardly noticed my own journey, the changing landscape and the new light. I was full of the girl, caught in the fate I imagined for her, and made my own. I had become her, in some way.

Before I even knew it, we had reached Chennai and it was time to get off.

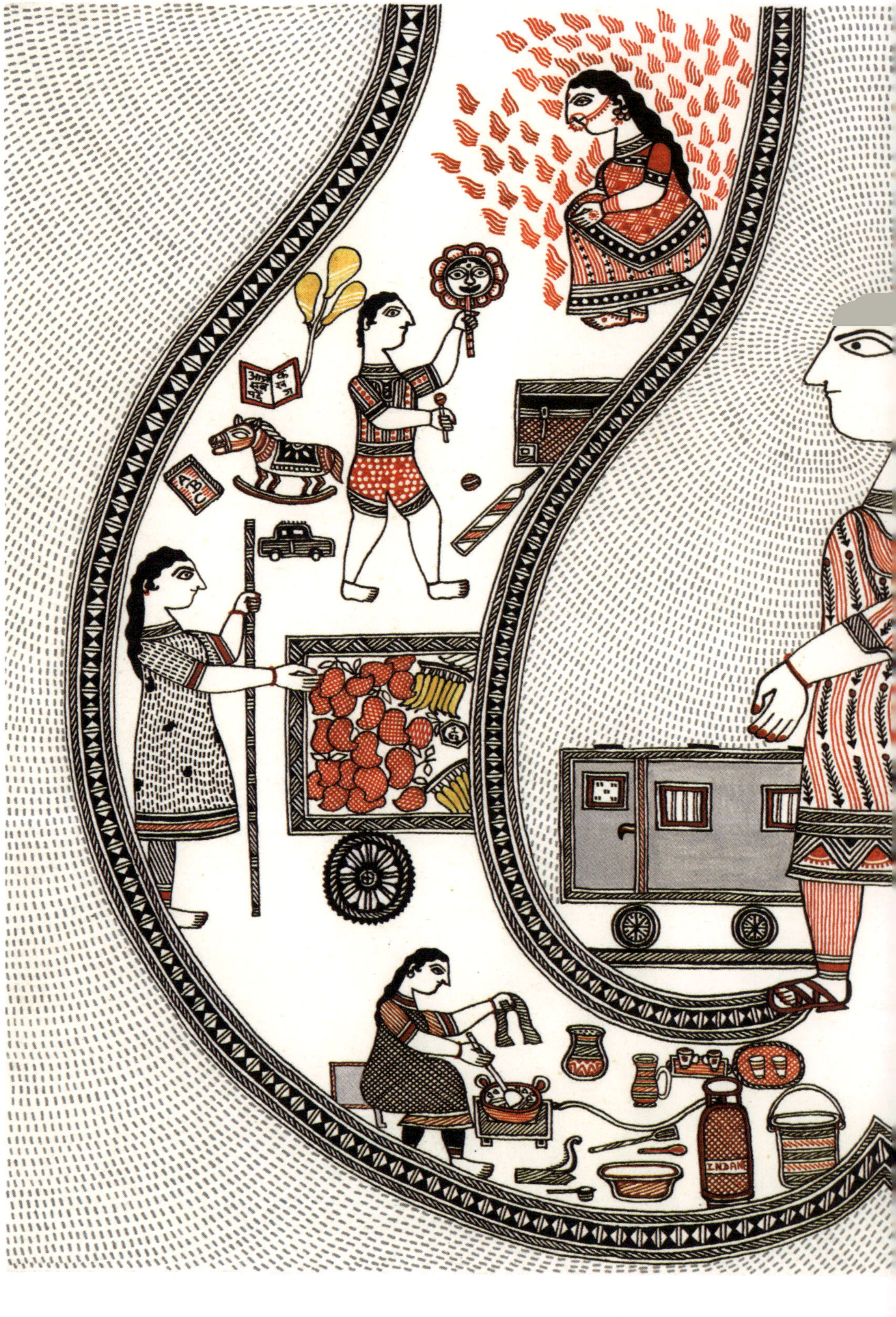

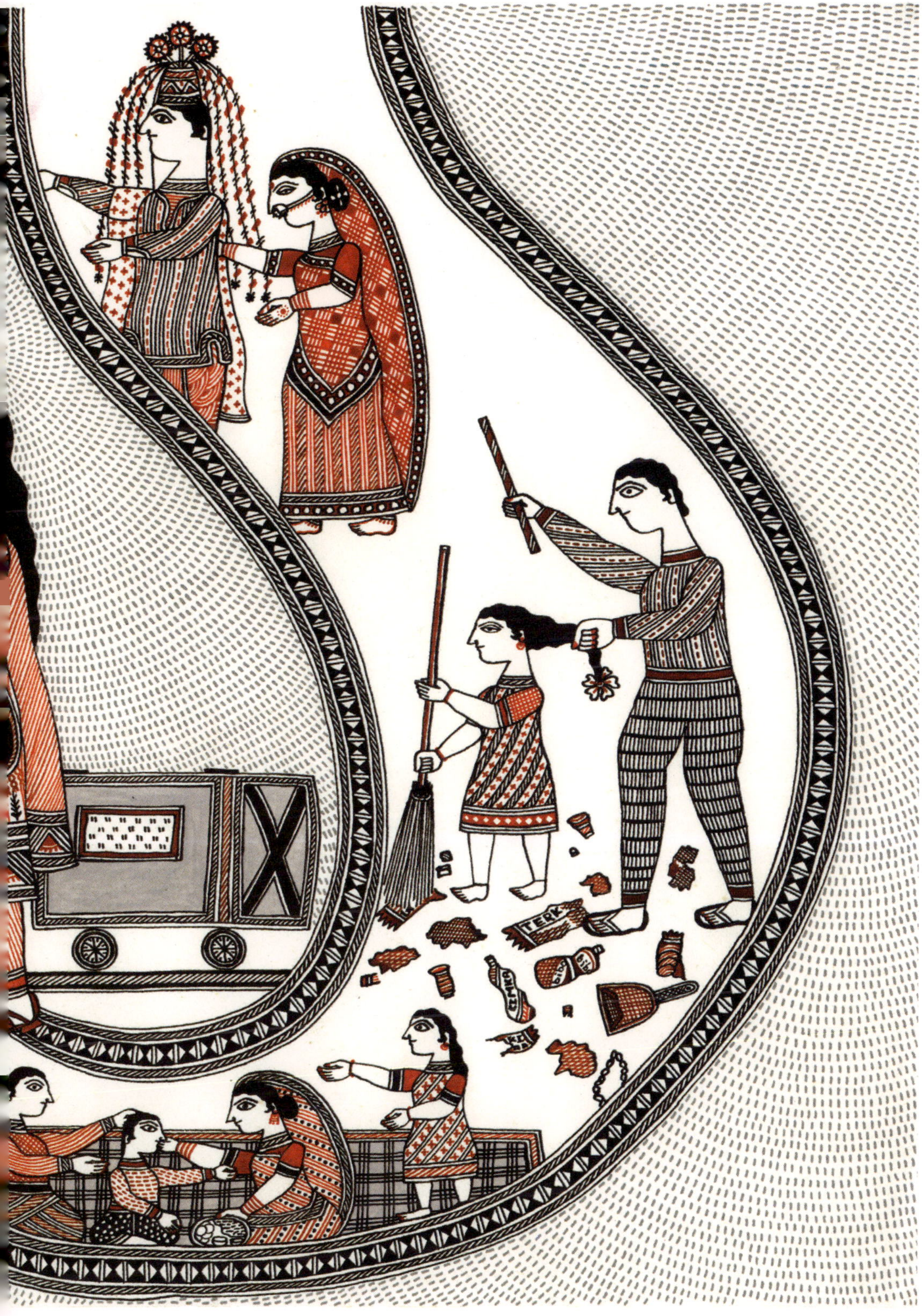

The girl with the sad eyes vanished even as I looked around. I turned to gather my things, and my heart was heavy.

Then, as I looked around, I saw a girl… and stopped in my tracks.

THIS OTHER GIRL was poor too, and her clothes were torn. She had lost a leg, but she managed to push her cart around confidently.

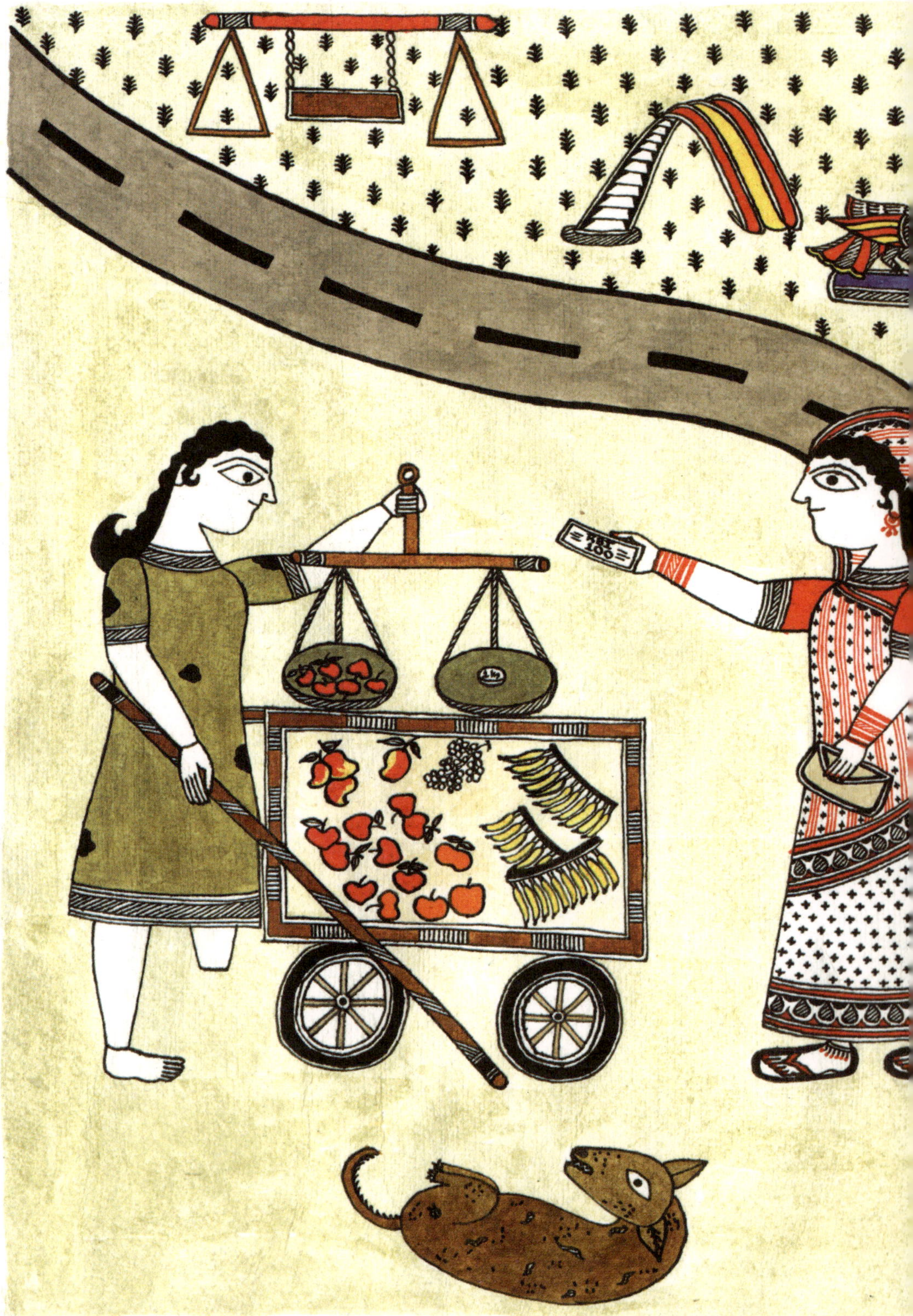

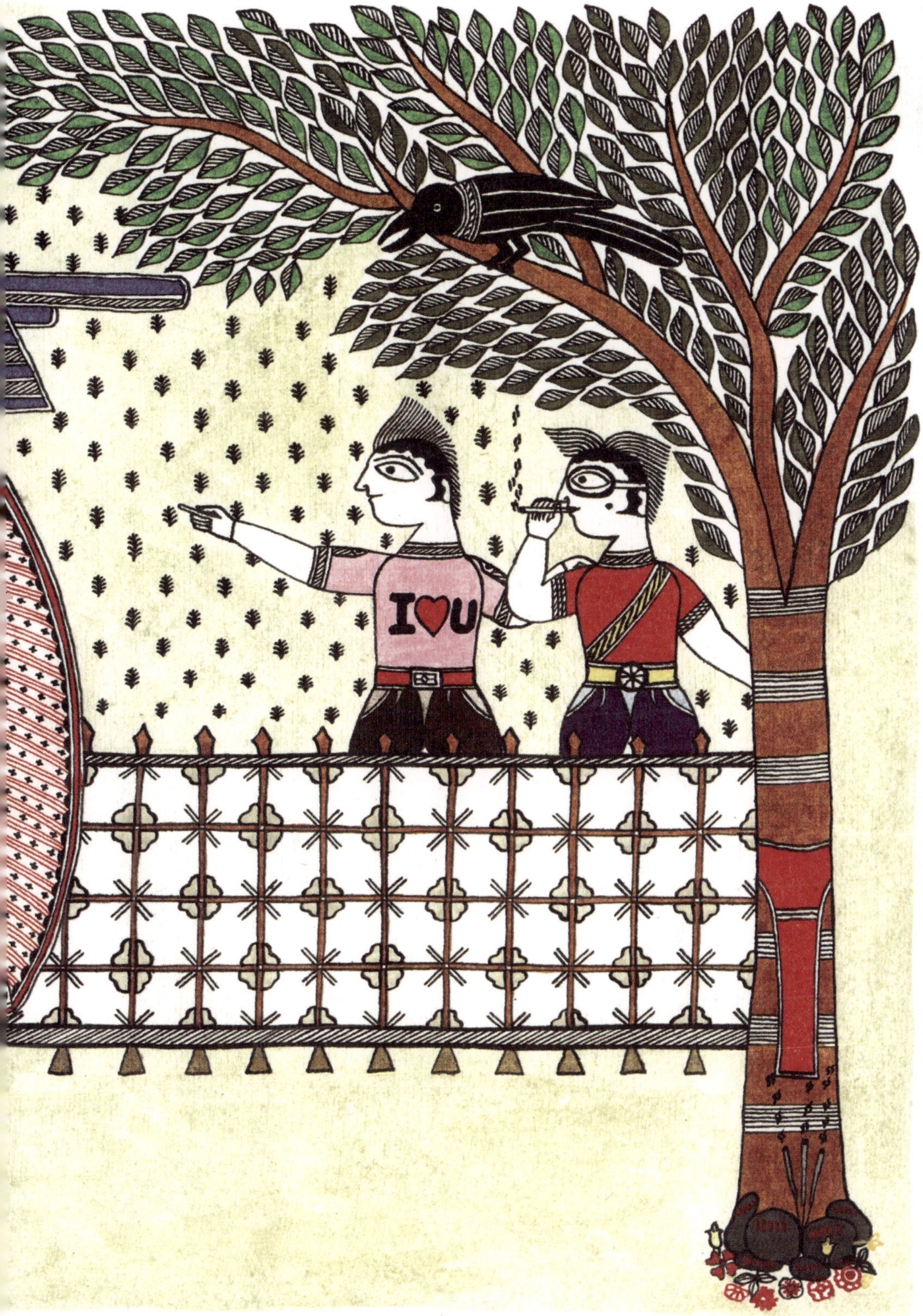

Two boys pointed to her and laughed, but she wasn't bothered. She spoke to her customers, counted out money, and weighed out fruit.

She's her own creature, I thought, she's walking around, she's earning and supporting her family.

THE SIGHT OF THIS GIRL, an ordinary sight really, still changed something deeply for me. My anguish for my sad travelling companion was no longer so sharp and confused.

I wish that things go well for her. We're all in this together, I remember thinking, lost, but not quite. We have to take what we have, go our own ways, and try to make the most of it.

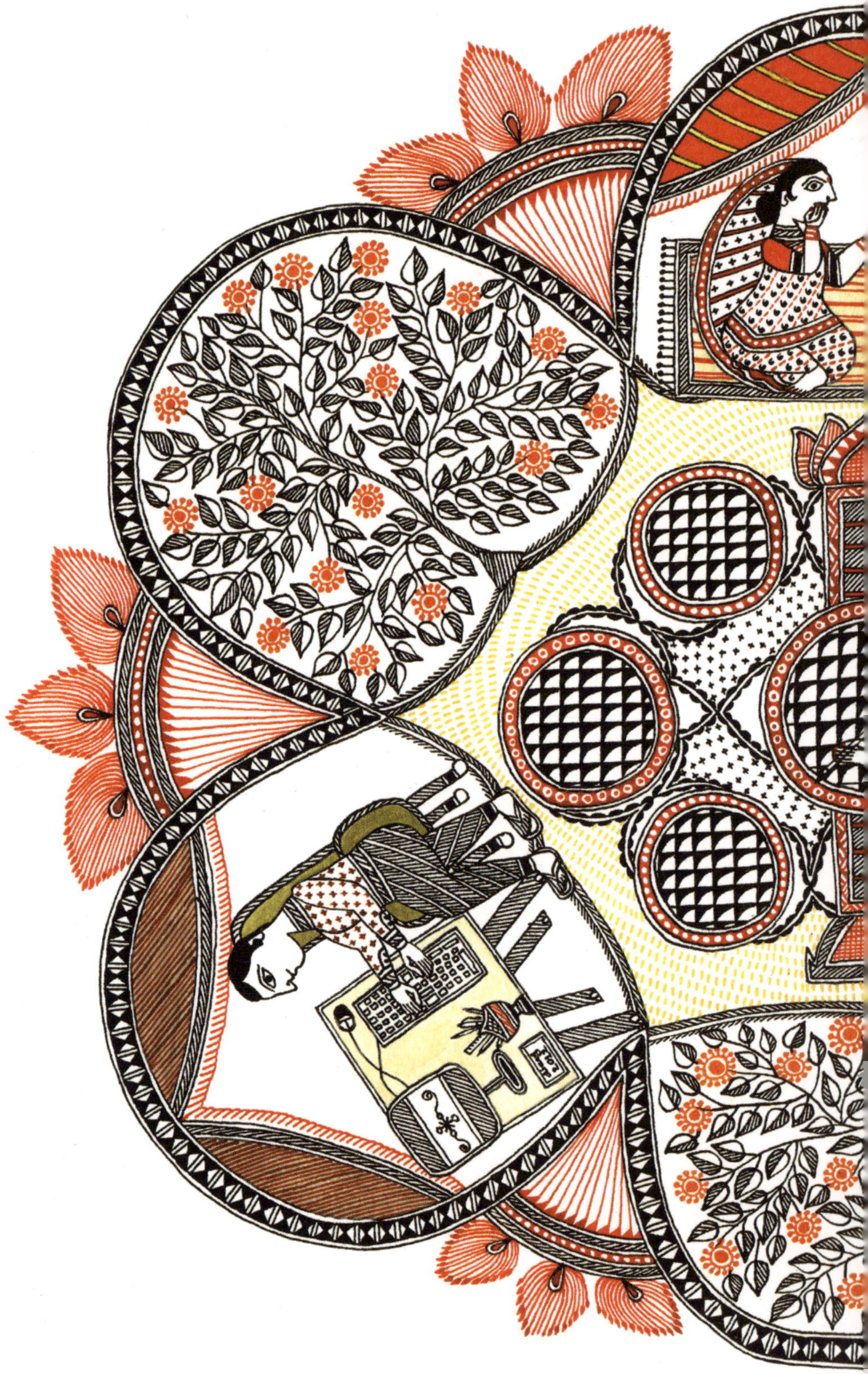

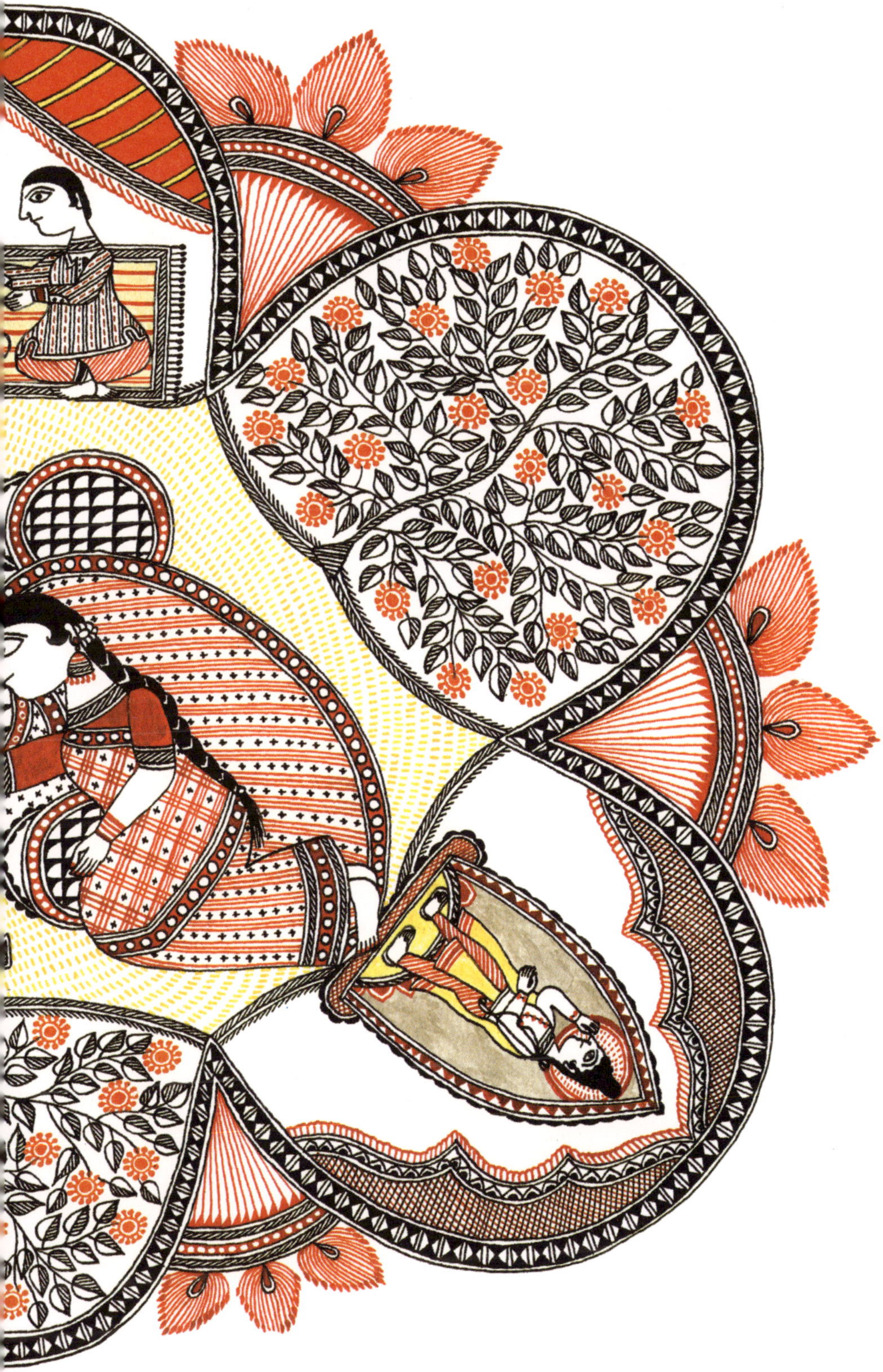

So here I am, having painted the story of a girl's journey, now imagining my own future as a woman. Some things are given, but it is a question of how life changes and how we walk into the future – I'm unsure, but unafraid, and I have some hope.

I want to be brave, and different.

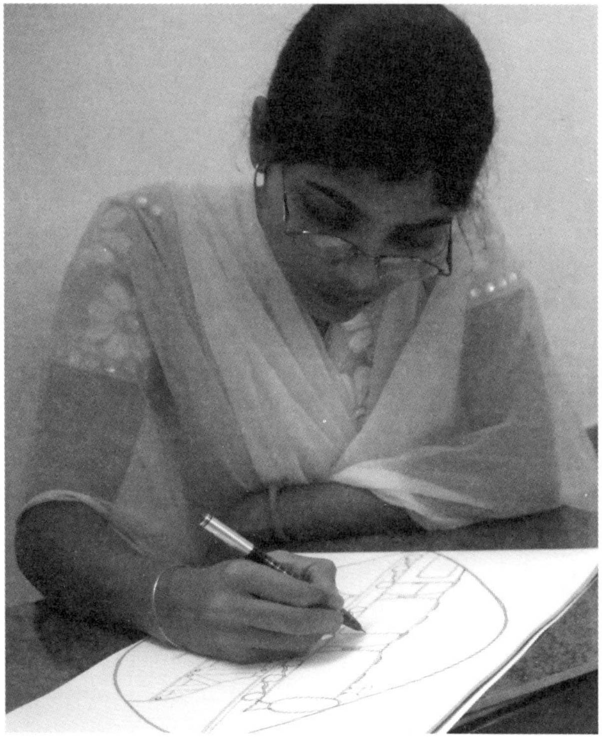

AMRITA'S JOURNEY

Amrita Das paints in the Mithila tradition of folk art, which originated from women living in rural communities in the state of Bihar. The practice in its original form – traditional designs and shamanic symbols painted on walls and floors of village homes – continues to flourish even today, especially during festivals and weddings. The basic Mithila style has several variations, depending on the region and the community or caste of the artists, but the different groups share a basic syntax and some common imagery.

Over the years, Mithila artists eager to take on themes beyond the traditional have adapted the conventions of their art form to new – and radical – ends. Young Amrita Das is such an artist. She was born into a highly patriarchal community, and has been passionate about exploring the reality of women's lives as far back as she can remember. It is fitting that this is the theme of her first book. The story is based on a real life incident, around which Amrita paints her reflective musings. The text is gentle, but it is also resolute: unflinching in the way it looks at the confines of women's lives, and persistent in its search for choices.

Her art treads a similar path between the known and the unknown. Delicate yet powerful, it retains the fineness of traditional rendering, while being conceptual in a very contemporary way. The art doesn't merely depict modern reality using the Mithila style of painting. Each image is a carefully constructed composition, and each one works as a kind of epiphany, initiated by simple, fairly commonplace events and experiences. Amrita uses a range of approaches to achieve her final effects: in the scene where the protagonist arrives at Chennai station, for instance, she chooses to frame the composition with two guardian angels – figures borrowed from a very different tradition of art – to add a sly and humorous layer of meaning. In other places her art works metaphorically, as in the image of train tracks – which stand in not only for the course of the journey, but also capture the protagonist's state of confusion and anxiety.

The Mithila tradition is by nature replete with symbolic forms and imagery, and Amrita chooses her arrangements carefully. She keeps within her inherited grammar of formalism and symmetry, even as she explores oblique possibilities to tell her story. Treading a fine balance between rootedness and exploration, she achieves an extraordinary outcome: she manages to steer her inherited tradition from the domesticity of its origins to actually question the traditional confines of women's lives. Her book is as much a tribute to women's creativity and self-awareness, as it is about their mobility and choices.

Gita Wolf
Tara Books

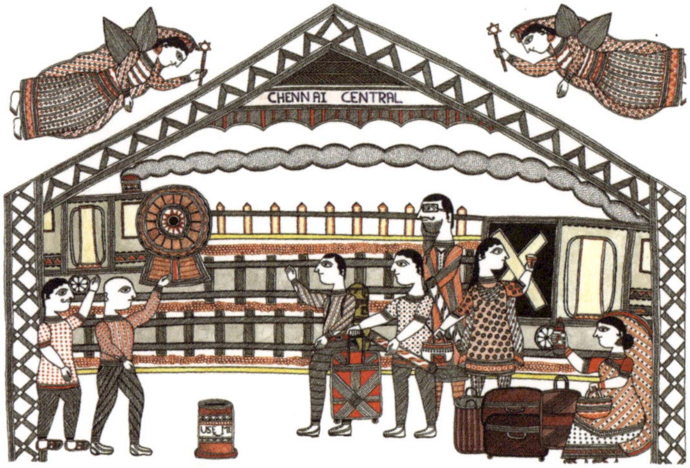
CHENNAI CENTRAL

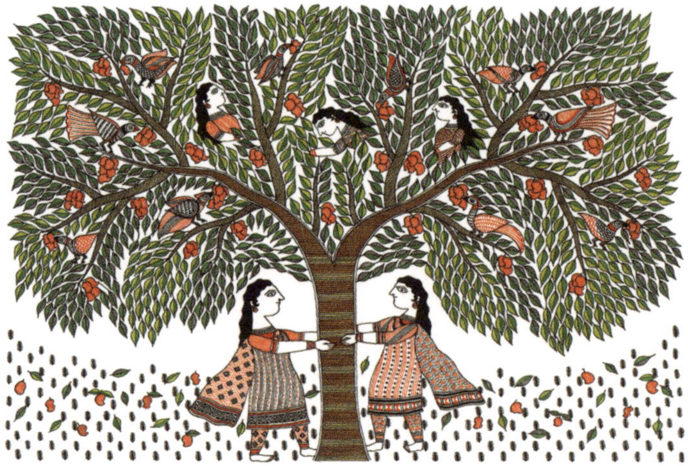

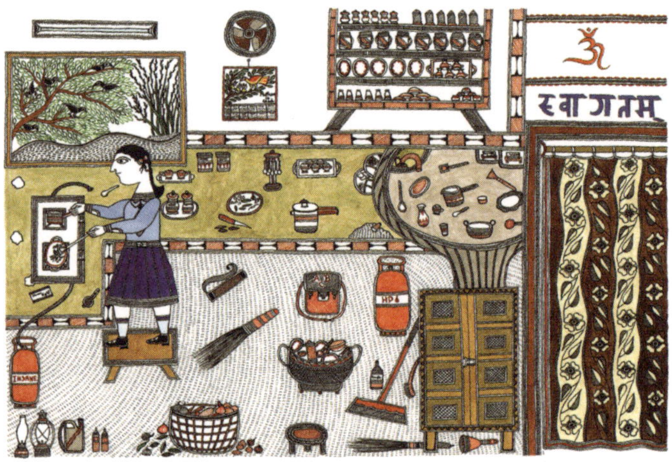
स्वागतम

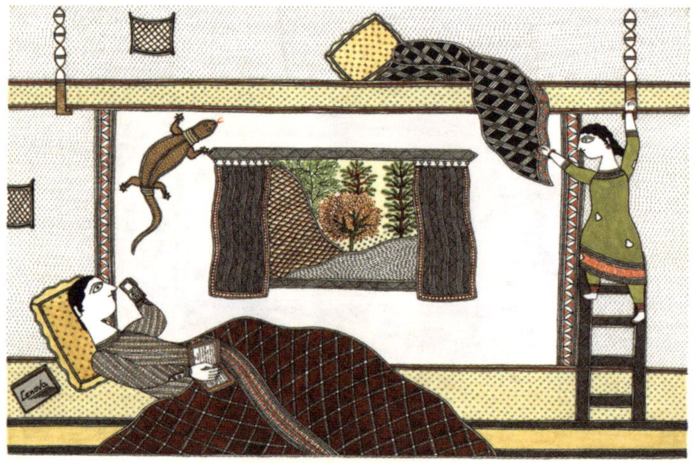

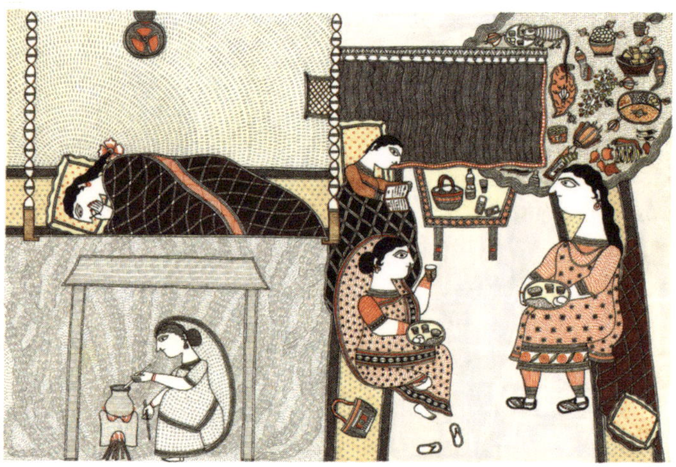

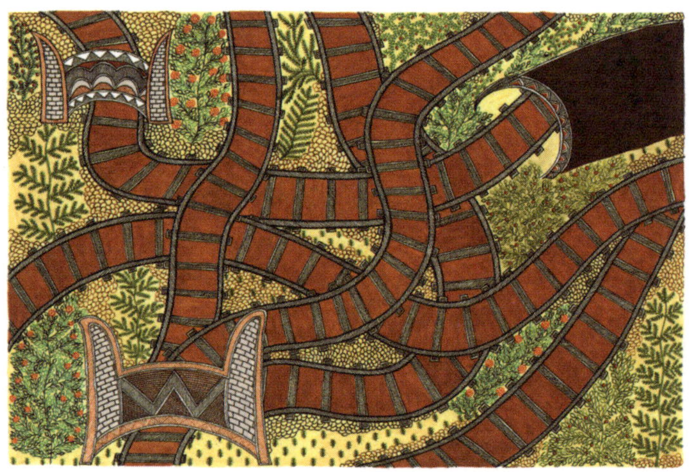

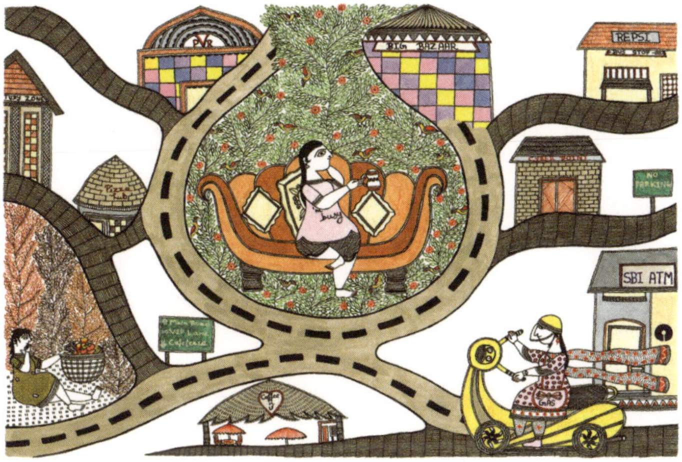
PVR
BIG BAZAAR
REPSI
NO PARKING
SBI ATM
busy
GAS

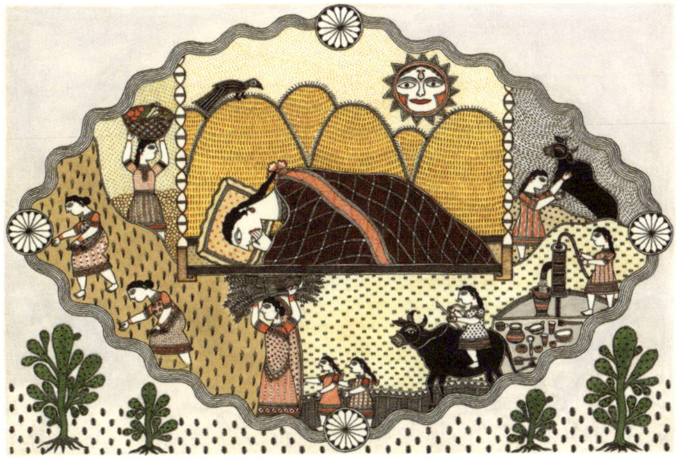

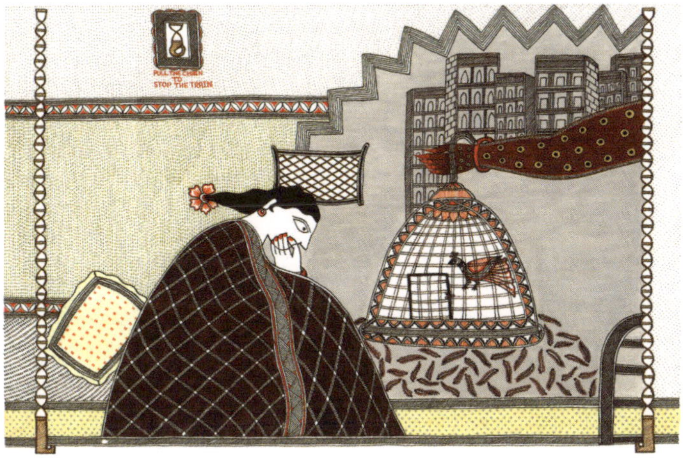
PULL THE CHAIN
TO
STOP THE TRAIN

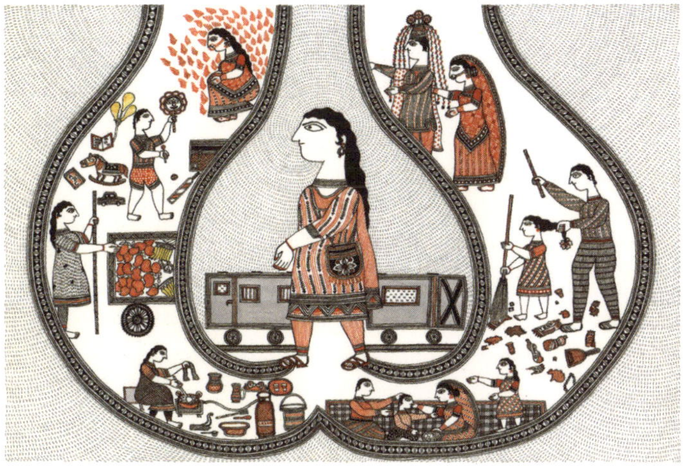

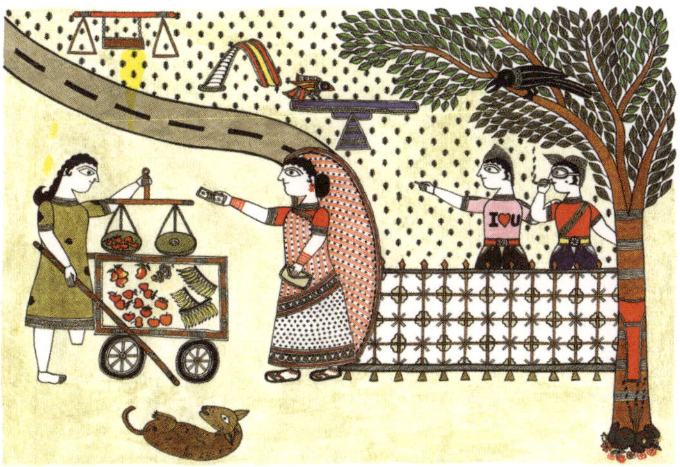
I ♥ U

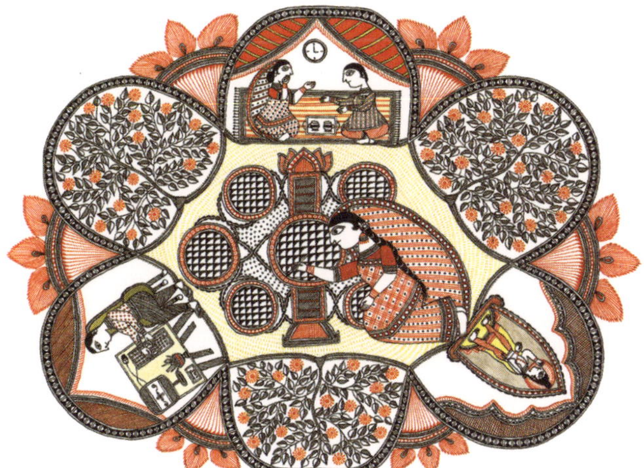

HOPE IS A GIRL SELLING FRUIT
Based on Amrita Das' original Hindi narrative
by Gita Wolf and Suseela Varadarajan

FOR THE TEXT AND THE ILLUSTRATIONS: Amrita Das

First edition 2013

FOR THIS EDITION
Tara Books Pvt. Ltd., India *www.tarabooks.com*
and Tara Publishing Ltd., UK *www.tarabooks.com/uk*

DESIGN Rathna Ramanathan, Minus 9 Design, *m9design.com*
PRODUCTION C. Arumugam

Printed in India by Canara Traders and Printers Pvt. Ltd.

ISBN: 978-81-939841-6-1